'I Am Not a Crook''

6/10

ART BUCHWALD

FOUNDED 1838

GPPS

"I Am Not a Crook"

G. P. Putnam's Sons
New York

Photo on title page courtesy the Washington *Post*
Second Impression
SBN: 399–11413–0
Library of Congress Catalog Card Number: 74–13501

PRINTED IN THE UNITED STATES OF AMERICA

"So, that is where the money came from. Let me just say this: I want to say this to the television audience—I made my mistakes, but in all of my years of public life, I have never profited, never profited from public service. I have earned every cent. And in all of my years of public life, I have never obstructed justice. And I think, too, that I could say that in my years of public life, that I welcome this kind of examination, because people have got to know whether or not their President is a crook. Well, I am not a crook. I have earned everything I have got."

—RICHARD M. NIXON
At Walt Disney World
November 17, 1973

Author's Note

THIS BOOK is belatedly dedicated to Richard M. Nixon, the 37th President of the United States, who provided me with more stories than any other man who ever lived in the White House.

Thanks to Watergate and the cover-up I had two glorious years of material, the likes of which I will never see again. From a humorous point of view, Mr. Nixon was a perfect President. Almost everything he did after the Watergate scandal broke lent itself to satire. The only problem I had during those months was that the White House kept topping me with their statements as to the President's role in this intriguing affair.

I shall miss him very much. If the truth be known, I needed Richard Nixon—a lot more than he needed me.

So, to Mr. Nixon, H. R. Haldeman, John Ehrlichman, Chuck Colson, John Mitchell, John Dean, Howard Hunt, G. Gordon Liddy, and all those wonderful people who gave us Watergate, I say thank you, thank you—from the bottom of my heart.

—ART BUCHWALD

Contents

IV. "ALICE IN WASHINGTON"

V. GAME PLAN

VI. SKELETONS IN THE CLOSET

"I Am Not a Crook"

I. THE JOINT RETURN

THE GHOST OF LYNDON B.

The ghost of Lyndon Johnson was raised by President Nixon at a press conference in Disney World. Mr. Nixon told AP managing editors it was Mr. Johnson who gave him the secret on how to get out of paying income taxes when you hold the highest office in the land.

My mind boggled as Mr. Nixon told why he paid hardly any taxes in 1970 and 1971, and I started to visualize President Johnson's last scene in the White House as Nixon would have us believe it.

"Wal, Dick, the office is your. It's a hard job, but ah know no matter what happens, you can tough it out."

"Thanks, Lyndon. Before you go, is there anything I should know about being President?"

"The most important thing ah learned as President, Dick, is if you play it smart, you don't have to pay any income taxes."

"But, Lyndon, I could never ask Americans to pay their fair share of taxes if I didn't pay mine."

"That's what ah've always admired about you, Dick.

You're an honest man. But the tax laws were written for *all* Americans—the rich and the poor, the great and the unknown. If you didn't take advantage of the tax loopholes, you would be putting yourself above everybody else, and people would say you think you're too good to take the tax deductions you're entitled to.''

"I never thought of that, Lyndon. I guess the popular thing to do would be *not* to take any deductions at all. But if I'm going to be President, I'm going to have to do the unpopular thing. And what would be more unpopular than the President paying hardly any income tax at all?''

"Now you're talking like a leader, Dick.''

"So what's the loophole, Lyndon?''

"You give your personal Presidential papers to the government, and they evaluate them for historical purposes. Then they give you the tax deduction which covers all the income taxes you'd have to pay while you're President.''

"But I don't have any Presidential papers, Lyndon.''

"You have your *Vice Presidential* papers.''

"Heck, Lyndon, they wouldn't be worth much. Who would put any value on a Vice President's papers?''

"Are you kidding, Dick? Your personal papers as Vice President are worth a fortune. Everyone wants to know how you conducted yourself in 1952, about your relations with Eisenhower, your trip to South America, your thoughts about your kitchen debate with Khrushchev. You're sitting on a gold mine.''

"Maybe you're right. How much do you think the IRS would give me for them?''

"Wal, ah'm not a tax man, but ah would guess your papers would be worth five hundred thousand dollars.''

"Gosh, Lyndon, that much?''

"At least. Don't forget you're now President of the United States, and no one in his right mind in the IRS is going to argue over what somebody says your papers are worth.''

"Well, Lyndon, if you think I should do it, then I will. I have always had great respect for your advice, and someday when they ask me why I didn't pay any taxes when I was President, I'm going to give you full credit for the whole idea.''

"That's mighty generous of you, Dick. Ah've always wanted to go down in history as the President who told his successor how to take advantage of our great American tax loopholes."

THEY ALL FEEL BETTER

Vice President Gerald Ford said on *Issues and Answers* that he expected Americans to "feel much better" after Mr. Nixon released his financial records to the press.

He did add that some people might continue to wonder if the President paid enough income tax.

I decided to make an informal survey among my acquaintances to find out if indeed they did feel better now that Mr. Nixon's finances are a matter of public record.

The first one I asked was a taxi driver. He confirmed Vice President Ford's statement.

"I feel great," he said as we were stuck in traffic on K Street. "I just discovered that I paid the *same* amount of taxes as the President of the United States."

"But he made a lot more money than you did," I said.

"That shows you," the cabdriver said, "that Nixon is a man of the people. Despite his friends, his position and his wealth, he still insists on paying the same taxes as a little guy like me. It proves he hasn't lost the common touch."

When I got to my office, I ran into a tax lawyer on my floor who also said he felt much better since Nixon released his financial statement. "Four new clients have called me this morning wanting to know why they had to pay capital gains on their property, and the President of the United States didn't."

"What did you tell them?" I asked him.

"I told them I didn't know, but if they wanted to pay me a thousand-dollar retainer, I could find out for them. Nixon's tax returns could be a boon for tax lawyers and accountants all over the country. He's shown us loopholes we never knew existed. I think he's a beautiful person."

I called Herringbone, a stockbroker, and asked him how he felt since the release of the Nixon tax papers.

"It's the best thing that's happened to me in the last two months," he replied.

"How's that?"

"Well, if you read his charitable deductions for 1972, Mr. Nixon, on an income of two hundred thousand dollars a year plus a fifty-thousand-dollar expense account, donated only two hundred and ninety-five dollars to charity."

"Why would that make you feel good?"

"I don't like to give to charity either, but I never had a good reason to refuse before. From now on, when someone hits me for a donation, I'll just say I'm budgeted for charity at two hundred and ninety-five dollars the same as the President of the United States. That should get people off my back."

Plato, my waiter, said he didn't feel as good as Jerry Ford thought he might. He has been having a running battle with the IRS over a hundred-and-fifty-dollar deduction he took on his uniforms. When Plato read that the President was going to let a joint Congressional committee on taxation decide if he had paid enough taxes, the waiter called IRS and suggested his problem also be turned over to Congress.

Plato's IRS agent said it could not be done. He told Plato, "Only a President of the United States can take his tax matters to the Congress."

"It gets me mad," said Plato, "because I have a better case than Nixon."

But Plato was the only one I talked to who didn't feel better since President Nixon has turned over his income tax returns.

Everyone else felt good.

As Doc Dalinsky, my druggist, said to me with pride, "Where else but in America could a man making two hundred and fifty thousand dollars annually have to pay only an average of five thousand nine hundred and sixty-nine dollars a year in income taxes?"

THE NIXON DONATION

President Richard Nixon is preparing to disclose that he and his wife will leave their home at 1600 Pennsylvania Avenue in Washington, D.C., to the American people.

The house, known as the White House, is one of the largest in Washington, D.C., and is considered one of the choice properties in the city.

A spokesman for the First Family said, "Although the President and Mrs. Nixon have not lived in it much, the White House has great sentimental value for them. By leaving it to the American people, the President hopes to take care of all the criticism leveled at him for the taxpayers' money he spent on his homes in Key Biscayne and San Clemente.

"The President's lawyers are now drawing up the papers which will provide that the Nixons can live there for several more years before turning it over to the government. There is some question in Congress as to whether this is legally possible."

The President made his decision to donate the White House to the American people long before the energy crisis, according to the spokesman, and he rejected media reports that the reason the Nixons are giving the White House to the nation is that it is too hard to heat.

The spokesman said also that President Nixon intends to include in the donation his entire tape collection which is considered one of the best in the entire land. These tapes, made over a five-year period, have been the envy of collectors everywhere, and while everyone from Archibald Cox to Judge Sirica has tried to acquire them, the Nixons feel they should stay in the White House where they belong.

The spokesman said that by donating their home at 1600 Pennsylvania Avenue, the Nixons were putting to rest unfounded rumors that Bebe Rebozo and Howard Hughes planned to develop the property for a forty-story hotel and a possible gambling casino.

"It's true," he said, "that plans were drawn up for such a project but the President rejected them when Mr. Hughes insisted that the Capitol be included in the deal."

Originally, the Nixons had planned to leave the White House to the Spiro Agnews, but something happened, no one knows exactly what, and the Agnews were cut out of the will.

It was rumored that the Jerry Fords might sublease the White House in 1974, but the spokesman denied this.

"The President has no plans to rent the house to anyone. For one thing, he has been informed by his lawyers that should he move out, he would have to pay state income taxes in California.

"Several people have offered to buy the White House, including Nelson Rockefeller, Ronald Reagan, John Connally and Teddy Kennedy, but the Nixons have turned down their offers. The price they offered was not even in the ball park considering all the improvements that have been made."

After the announcement was made, reporters checked with the Department of the Interior to ask them what they intended to do with the property. An official said, "We're not certain. For the last five years it's been run like Disneyland, and we'd like to keep the same flavor if we can. The White House should be a fun place for the American people where they can amuse themselves and forget about the cares of the world."

THE JOINT RETURN

"Hello, Dick. Why the long face?"

"I just got the word we owe four hundred and sixty-seven thousand dollars in back taxes, Pat."

"What do you mean *we* owe four hundred and sixty-seven thousand dollars?"

"You and I. You see, we filed a joint return because we're man and wife. So actually you only owe half—which comes to two hundred and thirty-three thousand five hundred dollars."

"Where am I going to get two hundred and thirty-three thousand five hundred dollars?"

"Look, Pat, I have my own problems. I can't worry about where you're going to find your half."

"I don't see why I have to pay half of your back taxes. You're the one who hired those stupid accountants who apparently didn't know what they were doing."

"Now, Pat, you're being unnecessarily harsh. They were only trying to save us taxes. Unfortunately they got caught in a technicality, and it cost us a half million dollars. After all, nobody's perfect."

"Dick, I don't like to say I told you so, but remember when you told me that we only had to pay seven hundred ninety-two dollars in 1970 and I said there was something cockeyed with those figures? You told me that all you were doing was what any American citizen is expected to do, which was to take full advantage of the tax laws.''

"I might have said that."

"Remember what I said to you?"

"No, I don't."

"I said, 'Dick, we could raise seven hundred ninety-two dollars, but it would be wrong.' It's on your tapes."

"Let's not bring up the tapes, Pat. I still feel that legally I did the right thing, but apparently the joint Congressional committee—and I'm not saying they don't have a right to—disagrees with us."

"I still think the President of the United States deserves better tax advice than you got."

"Listen, it wasn't my tax lawyers who screwed me up; it was Lyndon Baines Johnson. He was the one who told me I should give my Vice Presidential papers to the National Archives for a whopping write-off. At the time I thought he was just being a friend, but now I see it was his way of sabotaging me. He never did like me, Pat."

"What about all those other deductions on our apartment in New York City and San Clemente? Was that Johnson's fault, too?"

"That's just politics, Pat. They couldn't beat me at the polls, so they're getting back at me through capital gains. Every nickel we deducted was a legitimate item, and if it hadn't been for Watergate, we'd be getting a refund now."

"All right, Dick. Even if everything you say is true, where are we going to get four hundred and sixty-seven thousand dollars?"

"I was thinking of opening up San Clemente to the public. We could charge three dollars a person. People might come over from Disneyland. All the dukes do it in England."

"But that means we'd have to be there all the time, signing autographs. Don't you have any other ideas?"

"We could sell ambassadorships. I'm sure I could get one hundred thousand dollars for the Court of St. James's."

"You know they've been sold already, Dick. You can't sell them twice."

"Well, there is one other way of raising the money, but I hesitate to suggest it."

"What is it?"

"The Alka-Seltzer people have contacted me about you doing a TV commercial. All you would have to do is drink a glass of fizzy water, look into the camera and say, 'I can't believe we *owed* the whole thing.'"

A CHANGING LIFE-STYLE

A White House spokesman said that President Nixon's decision to pay almost a half million dollars in back taxes has "almost totally wiped out" Mr. Nixon financially.

If this is true, the President may have to make some dramatic changes in his life-style. These are the kind of stories we may be reading about Mr. Nixon in the next three years.

WASHINGTON—President Nixon gave a state dinner last night for Queen Elizabeth II at a McDonald's hamburger stand in Chevy Chase, Maryland. The President explained to the queen and Prince Philip that the White House was being redecorated and McDonald's was the only place he could rent on such short notice.

Entertainment for the evening was provided by Henry Mancini, Burt Bacharach, Peggy Lee, Glen Campbell and Johnny Cash records on a jukebox which was lent to the President for the evening.

Each guest was served one Big Mac and a bag of French fried potatoes. After dinner the President toasted the queen in Welch's grape juice and presented her with a Yo-Yo which was given to him by the Grand Ole Opry in Nashville, Tennessee.

Mrs. Nixon said she was looking forward to the dinner the British ambassador was giving the royal family on the following evening at the British embassy, as she was still hungry.

SAN CLEMENTE, CALIF.—President Nixon arrived here today on a Greyhound bus from Washington for the weekend. The trip took five days, and the President looked a little tired as he got off at the bus station in Laguna Beach. A press spokesman angrily denied that Mr. Nixon tried to get his daughters, Tricia and Julie, on the bus for half fare.

The spokesman said: "The President had been advised by his lawyers that if he traveled by bus, he was entitled to a family plan discount. When he was informed that this did not apply on weekends, he asked a joint Congressional committee on bus travel to look into the matter. Mr. Nixon said if he was wrong, he would pay Tricia and Julie's full fare."

WASHINGTON—The White House announced today that President Nixon would be going to Moscow next month for a summit meeting with Leonid Brezhnev. The President will be traveling on a charter flight with 175 barbers and their wives from Miami, Florida. The trip will cost $325, which includes hotel accommodations in the Soviet Union as well as continental breakfast. Because the package insists on double accommodations, the President will share a room with Henry Kissinger.

Mr. Nixon has been personally assured by Mr. Brezhnev that all gratuities, as well as transportation to and from the airport, are included in the price of the package.

WASHINGTON—Ronald Ziegler, the President's press secretary, announced the Nixons would hold a garage sale at the White House next Sunday. Besides Presidential papers and old tapes, the Nixons are offering other items of interest, including a cloth coat, a 16-millimeter print of *Patton* , an autographed football of the Miami Dolphins, three copies of *Six Crises* and several costumes left over from Tricia's masked ball.

The press secretary said that all items would be sold for cash, and all sales were final. Mr. Ziegler urged every American to attend this unique event, which he said may never be held by an American President again. There will be a $1 parking charge on the Mall.

THE NEEDIEST CASE

Mr. Maurice Dirk, a lifelong admirer of President Nixon, has just started a new organization called the Committee to Refinance the American President.

In his plush offices on Pennsylvania Avenue, Mr. Dirk told me, "From all indications President Nixon will have to pay anywhere from three hundred and fifty thousand to five hundred thousand dollars in back taxes—that is to say, money that he deducted which probably will be disallowed. Now to the average person that may not be much, but for the President this is a large sum of money. I think we, as Americans, should get together and pay the back taxes for him."

"I'm all for it, but how do we do it?" I asked.

"The easiest thing would be for Congress to pass a law making it possible for everyone filing a tax return to check off one dollar on *our* taxes to pay the President's penalties. In that way all the IRS would have to do is transfer the money from one account to the other."

"I'm not sure Congress would do that."

"Neither am I," Mr. Dirk said. "That's why I started the Committee to Refinance the American President. It would give companies such as ITT, Gulf and American Shipbuilding, as well as public interest groups like the American Milk Producers Industry and individuals like Robert Vesco a chance to show how much the Presidency means to them. It would be an opportunity for everyone to become directly involved with the President's tax problems and share in restoring our faith in the American system."

"There are some American people who might balk," I warned Dirk.

"They will until they realize what is at stake. The worst way you could cripple the American Presidency is to make the leaders of the nation pay back taxes. How can the President concentrate on the great problems of the world when the Internal Revenue Service puts a lien on his salary? Suppose the IRS decides to take San Clemente or Key Biscayne away from Mr. Nixon?

"If you make him pay back all the money the IRS says is due them, the President will have to change his life-style. He will be unable to give dinners for heads of state or Congressmen. He will have to cut out trips to Camp David. The IRS would put him on an allowance and that would be the end of taking his family to Trader Vic's. They might even make the President get rid of a couple of his dogs. You don't know how vindictive the IRS can be when they go after you."

"It makes you sick when you think of it," I said.

"The question the American people must ask themselves is: Do we want a poverty-stricken President who eventually will have to apply for welfare, or do we want one who is free of the tax burdens that affect the rest of us?"

"There is no question in my mind," I told Dirk.

"The Committee to Refinance the American President will launch a nationwide appeal this month to coincide with the 1974 tax season which, as you know, ends on April 15. We will ask Americans as they fill out their returns to remember Mr. Nixon's tax problems and to ask themselves not what the President can do for them but what they can do for the President."

"I'm sure you'll be oversubscribed," I said. "Does the President know you've started this organization?"

"No," said Dirk, "and everyone in the White House has orders not to tell him."

BEFORE WATERGATE

A group of us were sitting around the dining room table the other night when suddenly someone asked, "What did people talk about in this country before Watergate?"

There was shocked silence. It was hard for any of us to believe there was *anything* before Watergate.

"Didn't we talk about meat?" one of the men asked.

"I think we did," one of the ladies replied, "but I can't remember what we said about it."

"I believe it had to do with the price of it. Wasn't there something about a boycott?" someone added.

"That's correct," a man said. "We kept saying the price of steak was too high. But surely we talked about other things besides meat."

We all started wracking our brains.

"Wait a minute!" a friend shouted. "Wasn't there something about amnesty?"

"You mean for people involved in Watergate?"

"No, stupid, we talked about amnesty *before* Watergate. It had to do with draft dodgers."

"It's funny," a woman said, "I always get amnesty and immunity mixed up."

"So does the President. If it hadn't been for Watergate, Nixon planned to make a big issue of amnesty."

"I don't recall talking much about amnesty," another person said. "In our family we talked about how McGovern blew the election."

"Who's McGovern?" someone asked.

"He was the Democratic candidate who ran against Nixon in the election."

"What election?"

"The Presidential election of 1972. If it hadn't been for the election, we wouldn't have had a Watergate."

"Now it's coming back to me. McGovern ran with an Indian named Eaglefeather," a lady said.

"Eagleton," her husband corrected her. "And he wasn't an Indian. He was treated for shock."

"He was not treated *for* shock, he was treated *with* shock. That's why what's-his-name dropped him from the ticket."

"Well, then who ran with McGovern?"

Nobody at the table could remember.

"It wasn't Humphrey," a man said with assurance.

"And it wasn't Sparkman."

"Oh, well, it's not important. Say, I just remembered something we talked about before the Watergate—impounded funds. The President said he was impounding money Congress had allocated, and Congress said it was illegal. It was a pretty hot debate as I recall."

"Didn't we talk about what kind of FBI director Patrick Gray would make?"

"I thought the big argument was how much financial aid we should give to North Vietnam."

"They were great days," someone said nostalgically. "I wonder if we'll ever see the like again?"

"Do you think Watergate will be over before the football season starts?"

"Are you kidding? They're predicting it will go on for twenty years."

"That's a shame because I'm going to miss talking about the Redskins."

"Not as much as Nixon will."

"Let's make a pact not to talk about Watergate for the rest of the evening."

Everyone agreed. We ate our food silently. Finally someone asked, "Has anyone seen *Deep Throat?*"

No one had. We returned to our food. Every guest tried to think of another subject besides Watergate, but no one could come up with one.

So we all left hurriedly after coffee.

II. ALL THE KING'S MEN

SOMEONE IS TELLING THE TRUTH

It is obvious to anyone who watched the Watergate hearings that *someone* is telling the truth.

I talked to one of the members of Senator Sam Ervin's committee about this.

"We are naturally concerned, after hearing so many witnesses, that someone is *not* lying. But at this moment we are not prepared to say who it is," he told me.

"Surely," I said, "by this time you have some idea who the guilty person is."

"There has been so much conflict in stories that it would be unfair to accuse one person of telling the truth when all the facts are not yet in. I'm sure when our report comes out, we will cite the person who has told the truth and turn him over to the authorities."

"Why do you think someone appearing before a Senate investigating committee would tell the truth about his role in the Watergate?"

"Probably to protect himself. We knew when we started

this investigation that we would have to deal with the problem of someone telling the truth. When you're dealing with so many witnesses, you will always find one or two who are *not* going to perjure themselves. The committee's function is to discover who these people are."

"How can you know for sure?" I asked him.

"At the moment we can't. We have to listen to everyone. Naturally we have our suspicions that one or two of the witnesses have told the truth, but we need more than suspicion before we can take any action."

"Do you think John Mitchell was telling the truth?"

"I'd rather not discuss names at this time. You can do an awful lot of damage to a man's reputation if you accuse him of telling the truth to the Senate hearings."

"What about John Dean?"

"Please don't press me. If I name anyone who told the truth, it could prejudice the grand jury hearings. I'd just as soon leave it that the committee does have evidence that one or two of the witnesses have told the truth under oath, but until we get corroboration on this we have no intention of referring it to the Justice Department."

"Wouldn't you say your main problem in rooting out the person who told the truth is that most of the witnesses have had a problem recalling the events that took place before and after Watergate?"

"That would be correct. If someone says he doesn't remember a meeting or a conversation between the principals involved, that person could be lying or he could be telling the truth. We can't make judgments if a person says his memory has failed him. But where we can nail him is when we find him making a statement which is obviously factual."

"What puzzles me about the hearings," I said, "is that whether a witness seems to be lying or telling the truth, all the Senators on the committee congratulate him for his forthright testimony and willingness to cooperate. Why do they do this when they know some of the witnesses have been telling the truth from beginning to end?"

"I think it's a courtesy that every witness deserves. If you congratulate those who have been lying to you, you also should be courteous to the one or two who have been telling the truth."

"One last question. Do you think President Nixon has been telling the truth?"

"At this stage it would be unfair to accuse him of telling the truth."

"What happens if he tells the truth?"

"The Constitution provides that any President of the United States who tells the truth to the American people can be impeached by the House and tried by the Senate for high crimes against the government."

INVESTIGATING THE WEATHERMEN

After the Senate gets finished investigating the Watergate, I have another subject for them to delve into. And that is the weathermen on television who promise you a sunny weekend, and then it rains like hell. Here is how this investigation would go:

SENATOR: Please state your name and profession.

HARGILL: Archie Hargill. I am the weather forecaster for television station WFOG.

SENATOR: Now on July 27, according to your own statement, you predicted that there would be clear skies, warm and sunny weather. Do you have that statement in front of you?

HARGILL: Yes, sir. I may have said it, but I don't recall it.

SENATOR: Those remarks are in your handwriting?

HARGILL: That is correct.

SENATOR: Now, according to witnesses, it rained on both Saturday and Sunday of the weekend. Could you, in your own words, explain why you predicted a nice weekend?

HARGILL: I think we have to look at this in perspective. At that point in time I had received information from the Weather Bureau that a cold front was moving in from Canada. I assumed from this information, which I believed to be correct, that the weekend would be sunny.

SENATOR: Didn't you think you owed it to your viewers to go outside and check to see if it was raining?

HARGILL: In hindsight, that is probably what I should have done. But in the period we're talking about, I accepted the

Weather Bureau's assurances that this cold front would move in.

SENATOR: Now, when you realized you had made a mistake, why didn't you go back on the air and admit you had erred? Don't you think that would have been the decent thing to do?

HARGILL: I'm not sure. It could have cost the station a sponsor.

SENATOR: Are you trying to tell me that a sponsor is more important to you than the thousands of people who were making plans to go away for the weekend?

HARGILL: Senator, I believe you're putting words in my mouth.

SENATOR: Let's go back to your log for early July. You predicted, and I'm using your own words now, "great sailing weather and a blue sky from Boston to Nantucket."

HARGILL: I assume you're talking about the day there were hailstorms all across Cape Cod and a tornado on Martha's Vineyard.

SENATOR: That's the day.

HARGILL: I know this may sound strange, but I don't recall it.

SENATOR: When you found out about the hailstorms and tornado, why didn't you tell the president of your station? Don't you think he should have been informed about this catastrophe?

HARGILL: He was in Key Biscayne at the time; I did tell his administrative assistant that I thought something was fluky. But untill the tornado actually hit Martha's Vineyard, I had nothing more to go on than hearsay.

SENATOR: So, as far as you know, the president of the station did not hear of your forecast until the houses were wiped out by the tornado.

HARGILL'S LAWYER: Mr. Chairman, is this relevant to the hearings?

CHAIRMAN: In North Carolina we think it is.

SENATOR: One last question. How can we avoid bad weather reporting in the future? How can we keep young men like yourself from falling into the same trap of perjuring themselves before the television cameras every night? What I'm trying to say is: What advice would you give to other forecasters who are thinking of going into the same business?

HARGILL: I'd tell them to become disc jockeys instead.

"WOULD YOU BELIEVE?"

"Brothers and sisters of the Latter-day Disciples of the Church of Watergate, are you believers?"

"Amen, Richard. We believe."

"Do you believe I had nothing to do with Watergate and the cover-up?"

"We believe, we believe."

"And do you believe I knew nothing about the milk fund, the ITT merger or the Howard Hughes hundred-thousand-dollar donation?"

"Hallelujah, Richard. We believe."

"Now, brothers and sisters, I want to tell you about the tapes."

"Oh, tell us, Richard. Tell us all about the tapes."

"There were supposed to have been nine tapes. But when I counted them there were only seven. Do you believe that?"

"Glory be, Richard. We believe it."

"Do you know why there were only seven?"

"We know, Richard, but tell us again."

"There were only seven because two did not exist. The tape ran out on one, and the other was made on a phone that didn't have a recorder."

"Amen, Richard."

"Now would you believe I didn't know these tapes didn't exist until the weekend before I was supposed to turn them over to the courts?"

"We believe it, Richard. Bless you!"

"I know some people say I'm a sinner. . . ."

"No, Richard, you're not a sinner. We're sinners because we didn't believe you."

"And I know some people say I'm a crook. . . ."

"Only the devil would say that, Richard."

"And they say I didn't pay any income taxes, brothers and sisters. . . ."

"Who said that, Richard?"

"And they say I made money on my land in Key Biscayne and San Clemente. . . ."

"Amen."

"But let me tell you, brothers and sisters, when the record is out in the open . . . when the tapes are heard . . . when my side of the story is told, then you will know who the sinners are!"

"We'll wait, Richard."

"Now I know you're going to ask me about the eighteen minutes missing from one of the tapes."

"Tell us, Richard, about the eighteen minutes."

"Would you believe I don't know what was on those eighteen minutes missing from the tape?"

"We believe."

"Do you believe I'm being crucified by television and the press?"

"Say it isn't so, Richard."

"And would you believe those who don't want to crucify me want to impeach me?"

"Oh, Lordy, Lord, we believe."

"But, brothers and sisters, I am not going to quit."

"Let's all clap hands."

"Do you know why I'm not going to quit?"

"Tell us, Richard. Tell us why."

"If I told you, you wouldn't believe me."

ALL THE KING'S MEN

Once upon a time there was a king who ruled over a vast land from one ocean to another. Such was his power and wealth that he had a palace in the west, a palace in the east, a palace in the south, and on weekends he had one in the mountains.

The king surrounded himself with a motley group of courtiers who were not above stealing, lying and cheating to keep him on the throne. Many of the king's rich subjects were forced to pay tribute to the palace in exchange for special favors and goodwill.

Although the king knew what his courtiers were doing, he

shut his eyes to their behavior because being king was the most important thing in his life.

But, alas, one day the courtiers tried to take over a watergate, and this was too much, even for the docile people who inhabited the land.

The king, realizing his subjects were angry, issued a proclamation saying he was appalled by the corruption in his palace, and he would find the guilty people and banish them from his court forever.

He called in the king's prosecutor, an honest and devoted servant, and said, "I want to leave no stone unturned to find the people who have brought disgrace and shame on my kingdom."

The king's prosecutor asked, "Sire, does that mean I may investigate everyone in the palace?"

"Of course. What kind of king do you think I am that would prevent my own prosecutor from rooting out evil in the land?"

The prosecutor took the king at his word and started talking to the counselors in the palace. Each one had a different story to tell, and it was impossible for the prosecutor to know who was telling the truth.

He went back to the king and said, "Sire, we have heard many versions of the same story, but we have no proof as to which one is correct."

The king said angrily, "No proof? What kind of king's prosecutor are you if you cannot produce proof?"

"We know who has the proof."

"Then drag him here and pull his toenails out."

"This is difficult, sire," the prosecutor said, staring at the king's toenails. "If we could just have your scrolls recording your conversations with your counselors. . . ."

"Have you gone mad?" the king shouted. "I am the king. No one sees my scrolls. They shall go with me to my grave."

"Then," the prosecutor said, "it is impossible for me to find the guilty parties, sire."

"You fool," the king said. "My subjects are angered. If we allow corruption in the palace to go unpunished, they will try to throw me off my throne."

"But what can I do if you refuse to let me see the scrolls?"

"Let me think a minute," the king said. "If I do not produce the scrolls, the populace will *believe* I am trying to hide my guilt. But, on the other hand, if I produce the scrolls, they will *know* I'm guilty. Did any king ever face such a painful dilemma?"

"What is your decision, sire?"

"Alas, I have no choice," the king said. "Guards, take this man to the dungeon and chop off his head."

"But, sire," the poor prosecutor cried, "why me?"

"We can always get another king's prosecutor," was the reply, "but where can the people get another king?"

NATIONAL SECURITY

The only way to understand the issue of national security which Richard Nixon raised as his reason for employing his own superspies is to put yourself in his place.

Pretend for a moment that you are President of the United States. Despite all your dreams and hopes for this country, there are still people "out there" who are trying to "get" you. They could be students, blacks, Congressmen, Senators, newspapermen, labor leaders or just misguided souls who are trying to destroy the American way of life.

It is essential, if you are to be elected for a second term, to find out who your enemies are and what they're up to.

Unfortunately, the Constitution of the United States with its archaic Bill of Rights does not provide the President with the weapons he needs to find out who is trying to keep him from being reelected.

Yet as President of the United States it is your duty to find out if there is a conspiracy to keep you from serving four more years and to discover who is behind it. If some other political party took over the government, God knows what would happen to the country we all know and love.

So you do what any strong leader would do. You set up a unit in the White House to devote itself full time to finding out who the traitors are.

The group would involve itself in wiretapping, bugging, reading mail and breaking and entering the offices and homes of those people who are seeking to take away your rightful place in history. It may be against the law, but as President you have to deal with realities.

At first you authorize the CIA, FBI, Secret Service, National Security Agency and Justice Department to take over this illegal work. But when J. Edgar Hoover refuses to go along with the plan, you become angry and frustrated.

Here you are President of 200,000,000 people, architect of a generation of peace, leader of the richest, most well-fed country that has ever walked the face of the earth, and they won't even let you do a little bugging and burglary on the side.

So you say, "Nuts to Hoover. I'll hire my own plumbers to do the job."

You tell your staff to set it up, but keep your name out of it. You also instruct them not to tell you what they're doing in case the plan goes awry. But at the same time you want to know the names of those who are out to get you.

Once the plumbers go into operation you discover your wildest fears about national security are true. There is a plot to unseat you as President, planned and financed by the Democratic Party. You also discover there is another plot by Alabama's Governor George Wallace to do the same thing. Never has the country been in worse danger.

You discover through intelligence that the Democrats have set November 7, 1972, as the day they plan to overthrow your government.

You have no choice but to get the plumbers to step up their activities.

Everything is going swell, but then through rank stupidity which you have nothing to do with, some of your plumbers are caught at the Watergate. Now you have a real problem. You can either reveal to the nation why you set up the plumbers unit in the first place, or you can tell your staff to keep the White House out of it.

For national security reasons you choose the latter, hoping for the good of the country Watergate will go away. But because of a prying judge and an irresponsible press the story comes out.

It really gets you mad.

With new relevations coming out every day you are faced with three choices: (A) resign; (B) wait for impeachment; (C) tough it out.

If you were President of the United States, what would you do?

THE LINE OF SUCCESSION

Because of all the talk about impeachment and resignation, this country has suddenly taken a very careful look at the succession of the President of the United States.

According to the Constitution, as interpreted by the White House, only male heirs may succeed the President if for some reason he cannot carry out his duties. This eliminates Julie Eisenhower and Tricia Cox.

The nearest male heir to take over the Presidency would be Mr. Nixon's brother Donald, the Prince of Marriott as he is known at court. Donald is much more of a free spirit than his brother Richard.

Since he never thought he would ever assume the throne, Don has devoted himself more to the restaurant business, but people at the White House believe he would be a fair and honest ruler if duty called.

Next in line of succession would be Edward Nixon, the President's youngest brother, a dashing young aristocrat known as the Duke of Seattle. Edward has served his brother on very important missions, including picking up cash from the President's loyal subjects when no one else could be trusted with the job. Unlike his brothers, Edward has managed to stay out of the limelight, and it is not certain if he would have the mass appeal of Donald, who knows Howard Hughes personally.

After Edward comes President Nixon's nephew, Donald, Jr., known as Bonnie Prince Don to distinguish him from his father. There has been some talk that Donald, Sr., might step aside and persuade his brother Edward to give up rights to the throne, so his son, Bonnie Prince Don, could be crowned President.

Bonnie Prince Don, though still a young man, has had great experience in international relations working for Count Robert Vesco who was exiled to Costa Rica when he got into financial difficulties with the chancellor of the exchequer.

The one problem of Bonnie Prince Don's assuming the Presidency is that he is too young to serve, and a regent would have to be appointed to run the affairs of the country.

The nobleman most talked about to serve as regent is Bebe Rebozo who holds the title of the Duke of Biscayne.

The duke is probably the closest intimate of the Nixon family and has served the President by administering the vast landholdings that the Nixons have accumulated in the last five years.

But after Bonnie Prince Don, there are no more male heirs in line for the Presidency.

Therefore, someone would have to be found outside the Nixon family.

This might cause a great deal of consternation throughout the country, because it would be hard for anyone to agree on a President that did not come from the Nixon royal bloodline of succession.

There is some talk of changing the Constitution so that Julie Eisenhower could inherit the role in case her father abdicates, but the male chauvinists in Parliament have said they would never allow it.

A compromise candidate if none of the Nixon heirs could serve is Paul Delisle, the maître d'hôtel at the Sans Souci restaurant.

While he has no royal blood, he has served the aristocracy of Washington in and out of court for many years.

The country has never had a maître d'hôtel as President before, but the way things are going, many people have indicated they would be willing to give it a try.

THE FUTURE PRESIDENT

President Nixon's main defense against turning over documents and tapes to the House Judiciary Committee is that he is not trying to protect himself but the office of the Presidency. He has said he has to think of future Presidents when he makes these unpopular decisions to withhold evidence that under any other conditions he would be happy to turn over to Congress.

I think the President is right.

The year is 2001, and President Harley Finckley, who was overwhelmingly elected by the Radical Energy Party (both the Republican and Democratic parties had gone bankrupt during the Great Depression of 1983), is sitting in the Oval Office at the White House.

His most trusted legal adviser, John Dean IV, the son of John Dean III, comes in. "Mr. President, I must report to you that there is a cancer in your administration. There are people in your own White House family who are trying to mortally wound you."

"I'm glad you told me about that, John. What exactly is going on around here?"

"Well, do you remember last June when seven men broke into the offices of the United Constitutional Party at the Vesco Trade Center?"

"I think I saw something about it on television."

"They're threatening to talk about their connection with the Radical Energy Re-Election Committee unless we pay them hush money."

"How much would it cost, John?"

"Three trillion dollars."

"We could raise that, John. But it would be wrong,"

"Yes, sir, Mr. President. But if we don't hush them, they may talk about the ten-trillion-dollar contribution the nuclear energy producers gave to you to raise the price of uranium in the United States."

"I forgot about that."

"There's also the four-trillion-dollar contribution from ITT which was made the day before we agreed to let them buy General Motors, Chrysler and Ford."

"That's not my problem."

"But, sir, we have the meeting on television tape of the chairman of ITT handing you the money."

"What's it doing on television tape?"

"Don't you recall, sir, you ordered all the meetings in the White House to be televised for historical reasons?"

"I forgot about that."

"But the real thing we have to worry about is the break-in of the Washington Redskins' psychiatrist's office. Remember, sir, you wanted to take a look at the psychiatric profiles of the team before you bet on them?''

"Yes, I do remember that, and our people botched it up completely. They stole the records of the Washington Senators, and we haven't had a baseball team here for thirty years."

"I also have to warn you that they're looking into how you got the money to buy the island of Hawaii."

"I borrowed it like everybody else."

"And then there are your taxes. A lot of people cannot understand how on an annual income of twenty trillion dollars you paid only two dollars and fifty cents in income taxes for 1999."

"I donated all my piano music books to the National Archives."

"Yes, sir, Mr. President. But what should we do about hush money for the break-in of the Vesco Trade Center?"

"Do anything you have to do to save me."

"But suppose someone finds out?"

"What's the difference? They can't touch me."

"They can't?"

"Nope. Thanks to the foresight of the greatest constitutional President in American history, Richard M. Nixon. God knows what would have happened to this office if he had taken the easy way out."

THE HIGH PRICE OF DIPLOMACY

As everyone knows, the best way to become a U.S. ambassador is to contribute a large sum of money to the Presidental election campaign—and have your candidate win.

The last election was no different from elections past except that the prices of ambassadorships went up. Luxembourg, for example, never went for more than $50,000. But last year it was given to Mrs. Ruth Farkas of Alexander's Department Store, who made a $300,000 contribution to President Nixon's campaign.

Countries throughout the world are very sensitive to the

prices put on U.S. diplomatic posts and now consider it a matter of prestige if they get a U.S. ambassador who has made an enormous contribution to the Republican Party.

It was for this reason that the foreign minister of Zemululu called on an undersecretary of state here the other day.

"I understand you are sending us an ambassador who contributed only fifty thousand dollars to President Nixon's campaign. I want you to know my government considers this an insult. We deserve at least a hundred-thousand-dollar contributor."

The undersecretary replied, "Money isn't everything, Mr. Foreign Minister. The man we are sending you has excellent business qualifications and strong connections in the White House. He is held in high esteem by the President despite his paltry contribution."

"That is all well and good, Mr. Secretary, but I have it on highest authority that you are appointing an ambassador to Tonkidash who contributed a hundred thousand dollars. Why has the price on our American ambassador been so deflated?"

"Zemululu is in the malaria belt, and the climate is hot and sticky, Mr. Foreign Minister. We tried to get you a hundred-thousand-dollar contributor, but nobody wanted to go to your country. We were very fortunate to find you a fifty-thousand-dollar donor who didn't know where Zemululu was. We were so desperate we were considering sending you a professional diplomat."

"We would have refused him," the foreign minister said. "My government still does not understand how you can send a three-hundred-thousand-dollar donor to Luxembourg and a fifty-thousand-dollar one to us. Our country is five times the size of Luxembourg."

"You must understand, Mr. Foreign Minister, that size has nothing to do with our ambassadorial assignments. It is a question of geography. The big donors are partial to Europe and the Caribbean. When you give the kind of money they do, you can't expect them to take a hardship post."

"We still consider a fifty-thousand-dollar contributor unacceptable to us, particularly when the dollar has been devalued twice. We insist you find someone who gave at least seventy-five thousand dollars to President Nixon's victory."

"Mr. Foreign Minister, may I tell you something in utmost confidence?" the undersecretary said.

"Of course," replied the foreign minister.

"It is true that the ambassador we are sending you contributed only fifty thousand dollars publicly to President Nixon's campaign. But what nobody knows is that he also gave another hundred and fifty thousand in cash under the table. We cannot publicize this secret donation, but you, in fact, are getting a two-hundred-thousand-dollar American ambassador."

"How do I know you're not making this up?" the foreign minister asked suspiciously.

"The cash is in Maurice Stans' safe at the Committee for the Re-Election of the President. You can go there and look at it yourself."

FAREWELL TO CANDOR

When the White House announced an end to President Nixon's Operation Candor, the reason given for closing down the operation was that the President had laid to rest all the Watergate-related charges against him. With the release of the two white papers on ITT and the milk fund, the administration felt there were no further questions to be answered about Mr. Nixon's role in all the strange political happenings of 1973.

There was a certain amount of sadness in Washington when the White House made its announcement. Those most affected by the shutting down of Operation Candor were the special staff at the White House who had worked so hard to bring the truth to the American people.

I went over there to see how they were taking it. Some secretaries were crying; several press agents were cleaning out their desks. One Madison Avenue man was passing around champagne.

Herman Diogenes, who had headed up the operation, was shaking hands with his staff.

"Don't worry," he told a mimeograph operator, "if the President ever decides to tell the truth again, we'll call you back."

"What do you want me to do with this photograph of Rose Mary Woods showing how she erased the eighteen-and-a-half-minute tape?" a secretary asked.

"Throw it away," Diogenes said. "It served its purpose."

"Should I put these copies of the President's income tax returns in a file box?" another secretary asked.

"No, shred them. Someday some anti-Nixon historian might try to make something of them."

"What do you want me to do with this picture of Lincoln?" an office boy asked.

"Put it in the file box. We may need it again."

"It must be tough to close down an operation like this," I said to Diogenes.

"It breaks your heart," he replied. "Operation Candor will go down as one of the great achievements of the Nixon administration. We took a President whose credibility was at its lowest ebb, whose statements were being questioned every day, whose finances were muddied by conflicting evidence, and we proved he was not a crook."

"How did you do it?"

"By being completely frank with the American people. The President decided that certain questions of impropriety had to be answered. At Disney World he said he had never taken advantage of any of the usual tax gimmicks that most Americans use, such as cattle, real estate and interest. He told the governors there would be no more bombshells over Watergate, and except for the eighteen-and-a-half-minute hum on one tape, there were none. He said he would explain his dealings with ITT and the milk fund to everyone's satisfaction—and he did. Thanks to Operation Candor, the Roper Poll revealed last week, a whopping twenty-one percent of the American people do not believe that the President is guilty of any of the serious charges made against him."

"And you did all of that right here in this office?" I asked in amazement.

"I guess you could say that," Diogenes admitted. "But we couldn't have done it without the President. When you've got an impeccable product to sell, it's a lot easier. If you want the truth, we were victims of our own success. When I recruited this staff for Operation Candor, I thought it would take three years to refute all the terrible things that were being said about the President. You can imagine my surprise when it took only three months to lay every charge to rest."

"What do you plan to do now that Operation Candor is over?" I asked Diogenes.

"I think I'll go back to my old job."

"What's that?"

"Selling used cars."

PLAIN SPEAKING

One of the most successful books of the year is *Plain Speaking*, Merle Miller's interviews with Harry Truman when the former President was living in Independence, Missouri. Mr. Truman was quite frank about his opinions of the people he knew when he was President.

It is quite possible that twenty years from now someone like Merle Miller might take his tape recorder to San Clemente and interview former President Nixon on his eighty-first birthday.

It could go something like this.

Q. Mr. President, what do you consider was your greatest accomplishment when you were in the White House?

A. I kept them from getting the tapes. They did everything they could, but they never found them. Do you know where they were hidden?

Q. No, sir.

A. I had a pumpkin patch just behind the Rose Garden, and I hid the tapes in the pumpkins. I got the idea from Alger Hiss. (Laughter.)

Q. That was a great idea, Mr. President. Without the tapes, of course, they couldn't find any evidence to impeach you.

A. You can say that again. To this day no one has been able to find them. You know the special prosecutor is still asking for them. Every week someone serves me a subpoena. But I've ignored them all. If I've said it once I've said it a hundred times, twenty-two years of Watergate is enough.

Q. I noticed you were just served with a subpoena last week. What do you intend to do about it?

A. James St. Clair is in the next room writing an answer to it.

Q. Is he still working for you?

A. Yup, he's getting a little deaf, and his eyesight is not as good as it used to be, but he's still one heck of a lawyer. Anyone that can keep stringing along the House Judiciary Committee for two decades is my kind of man.

You see, the trick was never to say we wouldn't give them the tapes. The trick was to always say we were working on it, and we'd give them an answer in a few weeks.

It's been going on since 1974, and here we are in 1994, and they still haven't got what they've asked for.

Q. Next to keeping the House from getting the tapes, what do you consider your greatest accomplishment as President?

A. Paying my back income taxes. I want to tell you that was some blow when they asked me for a half million dollars. If I hadn't gone into the real estate business with Bebe Rebozo after I left the White House, I don't think I would ever have gotten even. But now that we've got the San Clemente Sun City for Senior Citizens and the Key Biscayne Singles Condominium Project, we're in fat city.

Q. How would you assess the people who worked for you?

A. They were the finest men I've ever known. Naturally I was sorry to see so many of them go to jail. But when you're President of the United States, you can't let personal emotions get involved in your decisions.

Q. What did you think of Jerry Ford?

A. I never trusted the man. He kept saying I should turn over all the evidence I had to the committee. You know something? I don't think he was as dumb as everyone said he was. He knew if I turned over the evidence, he'd become President.

Q. Mr. President, it's been eighteen years now since you left office. Is there one thing you would have done differently?

A. Yes. I would have advised George Allen of the Redskins to send Larry Brown off tackle, instead of having Billy Kilmer throw a pass to Charley Taylor in the Super Bowl.

COTTON PICKERS AT THE WHITE HOUSE

If anyone doubts we have a different kind of regime in the White House than we had before, I refer them to recent events.

Mel Laird, the President's chief adviser for domestic affairs, mentioned a possible tax raise in a press conference. An angry Secretary of the Treasury George Shultz complained that every time he left the country Laird gave a press conference on economic affairs. He said, and the world quoted him, "I think the President's adviser for domestic affairs should keep his cotton-picking hands off economic policy for a change."

Now the beauty of this exchange is that with the new team in the White House, George Shultz could say such a thing about the President's chief adviser for domestic affairs without fear of being bugged, burgled and banished by the President's top aides.

Had John Ehrlichman been in charge of domestic affairs the script might have been entirely different.

After Shultz held his press conference in Tokyo, Ehrlichman could have called up Charles Colson and asked, "What have we got on Shultz?"

"Nothing so far, except that he's the Secretary of the Treasury."

"Did you see what he said about me in Japan? He said I should keep my cotton-picking hands off the economy."

"What cheek! Should we put him on the enemy list?"

"We have to do more than that. I think this is a job for the plumbers."

"Egil, I want a psychiatric profile on George Shultz. Break into his psychiatrist's office and bring me back his files."

"Suppose he doesn't have a psychiatrist?"

"Then I'll call the CIA and tell them to make one up. This is a matter of urgent national security."

"How's that?"

"He called me a cotton picker."

"I got you, John. Let's go, plumbers. We have to save the country again."

"Miss Blatford, send in John Dean."

(Enter John Dean.)

"Dean, the President wants you to personally investigate George Shultz. I want to know where he goes at night, whom he sees and what he does when he isn't fighting inflation. After you get the information, go to Camp David and write up a full report."

"Yes, sir, John, I'll call Pat Gray right away and get the FBI on it."

"Also tap Shultz's telephone. He's trying to mortally wound me."

"Don't worry. I will launch the most thorough investigation in the history of the White House."

"Miss Blatford, get me Bob Haldeman."

"Bob, this is Ehrlichman. Did you see what Shultz said about me in Tokyo? . . . Right. Don't worry, I've already taken care of it. Dean is launching an investigation. . . . When we get the goods on Shultz, we'll leave him twisting slowly, slowly in the wind. Does the President know anything about Shultz's press conference on taxes? . . . Good. Don't tell him. . . . The less he knows about anything, the better it is for the country."

That might have been how it would have gone if John Ehrlichman had still been in charge of domestic affairs. But fortunately Mel Laird was running things in the White House and Shultz had nothing to fear. Thanks to a new mood in the administration, calling a White House aide a cotton picker was no longer considered a capital crime in Washington.

THERE IS NO NEW NIXON

I received a call the other night from a former White House aide whom I'll call Deep Toes. He said he had to meet me right away and he gave me the address of an abandoned garage in Chevy Chase.

When I arrived, he took me over to a wall, and we sat down on the hard cement. He lit a cigarette.

"I got something very important to tell you."

"What is it?" I said excitedly.

"You know you've been writing about the New Nixon and Old Nixon for the last five years? Well there is no New Nixon, and there never was."

"You've got to be kidding. I saw the New Nixon with my own eyes. The whole country saw him in 1969, 1970, 1971 and even 1972."

Deep Toes shook his head. "It was the Old Nixon with makeup on. We dyed his hair, powdered his cheeks and put him in new suits. We had everybody fooled. You were the biggest patsy of all. Any time we fed you something on the New Nixon you ate it up. We couldn't believe you'd be that stupid, but you were."

"Whose idea was it to put out the story there was a New Nixon?"

"Chuck Colson and John Dean cooked it up between them. They figured if they were going to resort to a lot of dirty stuff in Nixon's second term, it would be better to do it in the name of the New Nixon rather than the Old Nixon. You see, people would have been very wary if they thought the Old Nixon was running for office."

"What a damn fool I was," I said, hitting my head against the cement wall. "Was the President in on it?"

"Of course he was in on it. He played along with the whole thing. When he was in public, he was the New Nixon, but when he talked to us privately, he was the Old Nixon, cuss words and all."

"He sure did a good job," I said. "He could have gotten away with it, too, if it hadn't been for Watergate."

"What do you think the cover-up was all about?" Deep Toes said.

"The President wasn't worried about national security or the plumbers operation or Daniel Ellsberg. He was worried that Watergate would reveal that the Old Nixon was running the country. If it had come out before the election, he would have had a very tough time defeating George McGovern."

"I suppose so. But what proof do I have that there was no New Nixon, except for your word?"

Deep Toes lit another cigarette. "Who do you think cooked up the tax deductions, the real estate deals with Bebe Rebozo, the milk fund business? Only the Old Nixon knew how to deal with those problems."

"I forgot about that."

"Have you read the transcripts? Does that sound like a New Nixon? The Nixon on those tapes was the guy who shafted Jerry Voorhees and Helen Gahagan Douglas. When you hear them, you won't have any doubts about who has been running the country for the last five years. Look, don't feel bad, you weren't the only one who thought there was a New Nixon. Even Hugh Scott believed it until a few weeks ago."

"I guess you're right," I said. "But why are you telling me all this? This stuff could blow the President right out of the water."

Deep Toes took a drag on his cigarette. "I'm getting back at Bob Woodward and Carl Bernstein, the guys on the Washington *Post* who broke the Watergate story."

"What do you mean?"

"They promised that if I leaked the Watergate details to them, they would see that Robert Redford would play *me* in the movie. Now it turns out Redford is going to play Woodward. So I figured from now on, if I have anything good, I'm going to leak it to you. When you break the story that there never was a New Nixon, it's going to make Woodward and Bernstein look like a pair of incompetent stumblebums."

WHAT HAPPENS NEXT?

Everyone has his own theory as to what will happen to President Nixon. The obvious choices are impeachment, resignation or finish out his term. But there is still another choice, and while it is unthinkable, everything that's been happening is unthinkable and, therefore, cannot be ruled out.

General Al Haig comes into the Oval Office.

"Here are the latest Gallup and Harris polls. Only two percent of the people in the United States still believe you've told the whole story about Watergate. What really bothers me though is that there are no more 'undecideds.' "

"That does it," the President says. "Let's implement Operation Banana Republic."

"You mean the Eighty-second Airborne Division?"

"Get them up here by tonight. You have the plans. I want them to take over the Capitol, the Supreme Court, the Washington *Post* and all three television networks. I will make a speech tonight explaining what I've done."

"Yes, sir."

The President goes on television that night and says, "My fellow Americans, what I have to tell you tonight is of utmost importance to each and every one of you. Because of recent events including character assassination, lies, distortions and vindictiveness by the media, the Congress and my own Vice President, I have had to take action tonight which some of you may feel is extreme.

"I have promised you ever since the attacks on me that no matter what happened I would finish my term of office as President of the United States. Because of recent events I have decided the only way I can stay in office is by a military take-over of the government. It isn't an easy decision I make tonight. There are some, and they have a right to their opinion, who say that this is a violation of the Constitution. But I have been assured by my own Jesuit priest, Dr. McLaughlin, that what I am doing is not only legal, but necessary, if I intend to complete my term of office.

"I would like to end tonight, my fellow Americans, on a personal note. If you don't like what I'm doing, you can lump it."

The next morning General Haig comes into the Oval Office with a long face.

"What's the matter, Al?"

"Something's gone wrong, Mr. President."

"What do you mean? We had a military take-over, and not one drop of blood was spilled."

"Nobody believes that you've taken over the government."

"How can they not believe it? Isn't the Eighty-second Airborne all over the city?"

"No one is impressed. We did an overnight poll, and it turns out your credibility is so low that the people don't even buy it when you say you're taking over the government by force."

"But they've got to believe me," the President says angrily. "Don't they know I've arrested Congress?"

"I'm sorry, sir. It won't work. You can't have a military take-over if the people aren't convinced that you've done it. Everyone we've talked to says it's just one more way of you trying to cover up your involvement with Watergate."

Nixon hits his desk with his hand. "It's typical of my enemies. They won't even let me have a military coup. What do I do now?"

Haig hands the President a sheet of paper and says, "We have no choice."

"This says I'm going to resign because I can't govern effectively anymore?"

"That," says Haig, "people will believe."

III. PLEA BARGAINING ON THE POTOMAC

A "DEAR DICK" LETTER

A man in Leonia, New Jersey, writes, "If Richard Nixon did resign, whom would he resign to?"

It's a good question, and my legal counsel informs me that the President would send his letter of resignation to the Secretary of State, who happens at this point in time to be Henry Kissinger.

Mr. Kissinger could acknowledge the resignation with a formal receipt, but I hope he would enclose a letter of a more personal nature.

It could go something like this:

DEAR DICK,

All of us at good old USA, Inc., were saddened to hear that you were resigning. There is no doubt that you are going to leave a big hole in the government which even someone like Jerry Ford can't fill. But we understand your reasons for wanting to go. As you put it so succinctly in your letter, you would like to find something more challenging than just being

President of the United States. Although we hate to lose you, we can't stand in your way of climbing up the ladder to success.

We're going to miss your beaming smile, your warm sympathy for your fellow workers and your earthy language. I don't know anyone who called a spade a spade the way you did.

We're also going to miss the prayer breakfasts, the great state dinners, the trips to China and Moscow and San Clemente, not to mention those fun sessions in the Oval Office when you let down your hair and regaled us with stories about the Washington *Post*, the New York *Times*, the television networks and Chuck Colson.

I want you to know, Dick, that, thanks to you, the good old USA has never been in better shape. Our stock is at an all-time high, and although we've had to pass up a dividend this year, no one blames you. You didn't know about the oil crisis, and you certainly couldn't guess the rate of inflation, and surely it isn't your fault that the dollar is in trouble abroad. I don't think anyone could have foreseen the events, and I believe it was very unfair that a few disgruntled stockholders called for your resignation.

We also admired you for the way you handled your personal tax problems and real estate deals.

The feeling here at USA is that you did the right thing in taking the deductions, and they still haven't been able to prove that any of your real estate investments weren't on the up and up. I know they keep harping about the milk thing and the payments Howard Hughes made to your friends, but this is just jealousy on the part of people who wanted your job. You were smart to ignore them.

The gang would also like to thank you for hanging tough over the subpoena from Congress for your records. Heaven knows where USA would be today if they ever got hold of them.

As a small token of appreciation, the boys and girls in the office chipped in together and bought you a little gift which I'm sending over by messenger.

It's a brand-new Sony recording machine, self-activating, which we're sure will give you lots of pleasure. You could dictate your memoirs or use it to record conversations with your friends. (Heh, heh.)

In any case, every time you turn it on we hope you'll think of your long-suffering buddies here in Washington.

Nancy sends her best. Keep in touch, huh?
Sincerely,
HENRY KISSINGER
Secretary of State

A MOST GENEROUS OFFER

It looks as if there's going to be some hard bargaining between President Nixon's lawyer, James St. Clair, over the tapes and evidence the House Judiciary Committee has subpoenaed. While the President has said he was willing to cooperate fully with the House so we could put Watergate behind us, Mr. St. Clair as his defense lawyer has to think of protecting his client.

This is how the negotiating may go.

"Mr. Doar, this is James St. Clair. How's everything on the Hill?"

"Just fine, Mr. St. Clair. What's new at the White House that we should know about?"

"That's what I'm calling about. You guys didn't have to send us a subpoena. We promised we'd cooperate with you fully. When you voted a subpoena, it made it sound as if we were dragging our feet."

"I know."

"Now look, Doar, we want to be reasonable down here, and we're willing to give you everything you've asked for."

"You are?"

"Yes, with the only exception that it doesn't harm the Presidency or violate the Constitution. As Mr. Nixon's lawyer I believe I'm in the best position to know what is relevant to your impeachment hearings. I've sifted through every piece of evidence, and I give you my word a lot of the stuff you're requesting is not worth fighting for."

"How do we know that if we haven't heard the tapes?"

"I heard them, and the President's heard them, and H. R. Haldeman's heard them. Why can't you take our word for it that there is absolutely nothing on them that can contribute to Mr. Nixon's impeachment? What on earth would we have to gain by keeping evidence from your committee?"

"I'm certain, Mr. St. Clair, that what you say is true, but there are some members of the committee who have a thing about Presidential tapes. Now are you going to turn them over to us?"

"That's what I'm calling about. We're willing to give you forty-two tapes as requested."

"Then we don't have a problem."

"But the President feels he should have the right to decide what forty-two tapes to give you. That's only fair."

"I don't get you."

"The President is offering instead of the Kleindienst telephone conversation of April 15 a tape of his call to congratulate Don Shula of the Miami Dolphins for winning the Super Bowl. The President ways it's a much jazzier tape, and he's sure the entire House committee would enjoy it.

"He is also offering in place of his conversations with Haldeman and Ehrlichman on April 16, 1973, the complete unedited tape of his talk with David Eisenhower on February 12, 1969. He would like to substitute the Colson material you've asked for with a tape of a very funny meeting he had in the Oval Office with Miss Cherry Blossom of 1972.

"To show his good faith, the President has authorized me to turn over to you the tapes of all the prayer breakfasts at the White House, as well as a complete tape of Pearl Bailey singing 'When the Saints Go Marching In.' Furthermore, he is throwing in a tape of a personal message he dictated to Secretariat when he won the Triple Crown.

"He feels these tapes are something the House could play over and over again. Believe me, Mr. Doar, the ones you people have asked for are dull and repetitious, and you'd be bored to death. The ones we're offering you would give you hours of listening pleasure."

"Thanks, Mr. St. Clair, but no thanks. We still want the tapes we asked for."

"Okay, Doar. The President asked me to give you a message if you refused his generous offer."

"What is that?"

"He told me to tell you, 'That does it. No more Mr. Nice Guy.' "

CERTAIN CRIMES ARE UP

The good news in Washington recently was that crime had dropped in the capital by 50 percent. There was some question about the figures released because certain crimes committed in Washington were not included in the statistics. Had they been, the optimism about the decline might be considered premature.

Here are some of the crimes *not* reported in Washington in 1972:

Housebreaking at the Watergate Hotel was up 100 percent.

Illegal bugging of politicians increased 73 percent. While officials explained the upsurge in this crime was due to a Presidential election year, law-and-order advocates feel the rate of illegal bugging will continue because of the permissiveness of bleeding-heart Justice Department lawyers.

Acts of perjury in front of grand juries and Senate committees and in civil cases reached an all-time high, surpassing even the record made during the four years of the Harding administration.

Attempts to intimidate witnesses and obstruct justice were up 23 percent.

Destruction of subpoenaed documents and paper shredding of crucial evidence increased 33 percent.

The rape of public television continued unabated, and blackmail of TV station owners broke all previous records.

Administration assaults on the networks were up 43 percent over 1971.

Crimes of passion against newspaper correspondents hit new record highs, and the mugging of news sources tripled under the Nixon administration.

Armed robbery of the American taxpayer by the military-industrial complex showed a 34 percent rise over 1971—a previous record year for this type of crime. Because very few of the military-industrial complex holdups are reported, law-enforcement experts do not see any chance that this type of crime will go down. (When one government employee reported that Lockheed was robbing the public blind, he was immediately fired.)

Although more police have been added in Washington, pollution violators have been getting away with murder. It is now estimated that there are 14,901 unsolved pollution crimes on the books, with an average of 75 being committed every day.

While street crime was down, crimes associated with executive privilege were up by 13 percent.

Political fund-raising frauds also broke all records, but there have been no prosecutions by the government because of a shortage of watchdogs.

Illegal arrests of demonstrators were down, thanks to the end of the Vietnam War, but unconstitutional surveillance of American citizens continued to rise.

Bribery in the form of campaign contributions doubled during 1972, and the smuggling of cash contributions for immoral purposes across state lines increased by 74 percent.

Aggravated assaults on Congress by the President were up 54 percent, and premeditated vetoes of legislation broke all records.

While President Nixon has expressed concern with the increases in all types of crime, he still considers criticism of his administration the No. 1 crime in the country today. It has become so serious that he is studying the possibility of bringing back capital punishment.

PLEA BARGAINING ON THE POTOMAC

I was walking past the building where Leon Jaworski, the special prosecutor, has his offices when I noticed a long line which wound around the block.

"What's going on?" I asked a police officer who was making sure that the people were orderly.

"They're Watergate defendants and their lawyers, and they're waiting to plea bargain with the special prosecutor. It's getting near deadline time, and I guess some of them are getting nervous."

I went up to one of the men standing in line.

"How's it going?"

He referred the question to the man standing next to him who was carrying a briefcase. It was his lawyer.

"My client just remembered that he withheld some information from the grand jury that he forgot. We wish to make amends by cooperating in any way we can with the special prosecutor."

"What do you hope to get out of it?"

"Thirty days and an electric toaster."

"A toaster? Is the special prosecutor giving out premiums?"

"Of course," the lawyer replied. "How else would he get anyone to plea bargain? I know one defendant who perjured himself in front of a Senate committee and he got a six months' suspended sentence and a set of Arnold Palmer golf clubs."

The line was moving slowly. A defendant and his lawyer came out of the building. The defendant was smiling.

"What did you get?" someone yelled.

"Ten months on a prison farm and an electric blanket," the defendant shouted happily.

"The lucky stiff," a man in the line said. "By the time we get upstairs they'll be out of electric blankets."

"Did you hear," another man in the line said, "that if you turn in a friend and they keep him deposited for a year, you're entitled to a color television set?"

"Wow," said somebody. "I could get two TV sets today."

A defendant and his lawyer tried to break in the line. Everyone started yelling. "Get in the back! Get in the back!"

The lawyer said, "My client is being indicted in Los Angeles this afternoon, and we have to catch a plane."

"Tough luck," a lawyer shouted. "You should have plea bargained last week."

"We couldn't. He was indicted in New York last week. And next week he's being indicted in Florida. This is the only spare time we've got."

Everyone grumbled, but they let them stay.

A defendant came out carrying a silver tea set.

"How did you get that?" a lawyer asked.

"I pleaded guilty to obstruction of justice and promised to implicate a former Attorney General of the United States. So they offered me ninety days and a choice of a tea set or a set of Elvis Presley records."

The policeman came by and cut off the line. "I'm sorry, I've been ordered to cut the line here. That's all the plea bargaining they can handle today. The rest of you have to come back tomorrow."

"Damn," said a defendant in the back of the line, "I think I'll plead not guilty."

"I can't let you do it," his lawyer said. "I promised my wife I'd bring home a set of Tupperware."

THE CLASS ACTION SUIT

The big story in Washington recently was the revelation that the White House had an official "enemies" list which they intended to use to "get" the people who opposed the administration.

Naturally, anyone worth his salt in this town was hoping to make the list. The test of one's importance in Washington obviously depends on how seriously the White House takes you and to what lengths they would go, to use a John Dean word, to "screw" you.

When the list was released, I searched it frantically for my name. First there was the "Dirty Twenty." I didn't make it, so I waited for the second list of 200 and discovered I hadn't made that one either. I thought to myself, "What kind of people do we have in the White House who don't even know who their *real* enemies are?"

Then the phone started to ring. Friends called to give their condolences. Sources who had been leaking to me on a steady basis telephoned to say they hadn't realized for the past five years that they had been leaking to a nobody. Colleagues who made the enemy list stopped by the office to rub in the fact that I was finished as a serious communicator.

Bill Mauldin telephoned from Chicago. He also hadn't made the list. Pat Oliphant checked in from Denver because he was left off. Paul Conrad of the Los Angeles *Times* was furious because they hadn't mentioned him. Herb Block said, "That does it for me. No more Mr. Nice Guy."

The worst blow came at lunch time when I went to the Sans Souci restaurant and found myself sitting next to the kitchen. The maître d'hôtel, working from the "list," was seating all the White House enemies at the best tables.

When I protested about the table, Paul said, "You're lucky to be here at all. With all the enemies the White House has, I can no longer let in every Art, Dick and Harry."

I must say my wife took it well. "You may not be an enemy to them," she said, kissing me on the cheek when I walked in, "but you're still an enemy to me."

That night I studied the list again. It seemed to be filled with such mediocre people. Then suddenly it dawned on me! The White House knew exactly what they were doing. These thugs and double-crossing, lying rats (names on request with a self-addressed envelope) had drawn up the list not to get the people on it, but to get the people who were left *off* it.

They knew the best way to "screw" their real enemies was by leaving them off the most prestigious list in the United States today.

By not mentioning us, they knew editors and TV executives would lose faith in us and find ways of putting us out of business.

"What a Machiavellian plan," I said to myself. "Why did it take me so long to realize it?"

I immediately called Block, Mauldin, Oliphant and Conrad and told them what the White House was up to.

We decided there was only one thing to do. We will immediately institute a class action suit against the White House, John Dean III, Charles Colson, Bob Haldeman, John Ehrlichman and possibly the President of the United States, on behalf of all the people in the United States who did not make the official enemies list.

We intend to prove we were financially damaged and publicly humiliated and suffered grievous professional injury. We will prove that the White House conspired to put out a straw man list of names to detract from their real enemies in the media, the arts, the Congress and the business world.

We only hope Maurice Stans has enough money in his safe to pay for the damages we are certain will be awarded to us. If not, we intend to attach certain homes in Key Biscayne and San Clemente.

THE BOOMING LAW BUSINESS

This has probably been the greatest year in history for criminal lawyers. Thanks to the Watergate fallout, every law firm in this city is now on a twenty-four-hour, seven-day week schedule. Whereas most law offices were sedate, quiet places, they now resemble brokerage offices with everyone screaming into the phones.

I stopped in to see a friend of mine who works for one of the top criminal law firms in Washington. He had his coat off, his shirt open at the collar, his tie askew, and he was writing furiously on a yellow pad. He motioned for me to sit down. Then he yelled into the phone, "Right, I got you. Forty-three indictments in Jersey. We'll take them. Tell them to put the money in the bank." He hung up.

"Boy, what a day," he told me. "I just—" The phone rang. "Yeah . . . yeah . . . we take perjury. How many cases you got? . . . Fifteen . . . grand jury or Senate? . . . Both . . . Okay . . . Send them over. No, not today. . . . We can't see them for two weeks. . . . You can't wait that long? . . . So get yourself another lawyer." He hung up.

"You really must be doing well to turn away business."

"Every time someone gets indicted he wants to see his lawyer *right away*. They'll call back. Most law firms have a one-month waiting list for perjurers."

My friend's secretary came in. "Mr. McIntosh, we have a mayor outside who is being indicted for income tax evasion."

"Tell him we don't take mayors anymore. You have to be either a president of a corporation or a high official of the administration."

A law partner rushed in. "We've been offered three hundred bribery cases in Baltimore County. Should we take them?"

"Take two hundred," my friend shouted. "We can't put all our eggs in bribery."

"What price should I quote?"

"One hundred thousand a case in advance, two hundred thousand before we go to trial. Vote fraud is fifty thousand extra."

"Wow," I said, "you people are really raking in the money."

"Watergate's been very good to us," my friend said. "You know, before Watergate all we got were a lot of priests and students being indicted by the government. Most of them didn't have a dime. But now you're getting a much higher class of defendant. They come from the best families, they went to the best schools, and they all have short hair. Most of the people being indicted these days are lawyers, so you don't have to explain things to them twice. I tell you it's a pleasure doing business with them."

The phone rang. He picked it up. "Oh, hi, Buzz. You offering us forty-three kickback cases in New York? Sure, we'll take them if your law firm doesn't want them. . . . I see you have sixty-three judges coming up for trial. . . . Look, while I have you on the phone, would you take thirty-three wiretapping trials in Los Angeles? We just don't have the troops to send to L.A. . . . Thanks a lot. . . ."

The secretary came back in. "There's a delegation of ex-White House aides to see you. They say it's very important."

"Send them to the White House department down on the second floor."

Another law partner came in. "You interested in a former Attorney General and a former Secretary of Commerce?"

"Good God," my friend said in exasperation, "I've only got two hands."

The phone buzzed. He picked it up.

"Oh, yes, sir, Mr. Vice President. Uh-huh . . . uh-huh. . . . Yes I've been reading about it in the newspapers. . . . I see. . . . Well we usually don't handle Vice Presidents, but we might make an exception in your case. . . . Now could you start at the beginning? . . ."

THE PRESIDENT'S BROTHER

The startling revelation that President Nixon had tapped the telephone of his own brother, F. Donald Nixon, has caused great concern among civil libertarians. If a President can tap his own brother without a court order, their thinking goes, no one in this country is safe.

But there is a school of legal opinion that maintains the Fourth Amendment guarantees of right of privacy and of protection against search and seizure do not cover blood relatives of high government officials.

The leader of this school is the great constitutional lawyer Professor Sam Clemente, who wrote the definitive book on President Millard Fillmore's wiretapping activities, titled *He Ain't Heavy, He's My Brother.*

Professor Clemente told me, "The Supreme Court has ruled on many occasions that it is perfectly legal for a President to tap his brother's telephone in the interests of national security. In the case of President Fillmore, the President suspected his brother Dillard was getting kickbacks from slaves who were working on government projects in the South. Fillmore ordered the Secret Service to tap his brother's lines.

When the Washington *Post* broke the story, Fillmore's press secretary announced the tap had been placed on Dillard because of threats on his life. Most of the threats were made by President Fillmore himself. But when questioned about this, the press secretary refused to comment.

"Fillmore's brother sued the President for invasion of privacy but the Supreme Court, in a five to four decision, ruled in the President's favor. The majority opinion said, 'It is obvious that writers of the Constitution did not have relatives in mind when they wrote the Fourth Amendment. It is impossible for a President of the United States to carry on his executive duties without knowing what his brother is up to.

"'Nobody can do more damage to a President than his brother, and since most brothers tend to take advantage of the President's high office, it is essential that the President of the United States be given free rein to tap his kinfolk.'"

Clemente continued, "But the court ruled that the President could not tap in-laws. 'We realize,' the ruling said, 'that in many cases a brother-in-law could give a President even more trouble than a brother. But if we opened the privilege to brothers-in-law, there would be no end to wiretapping in this country.'

"Although President Fillmore won the suit, he agreed not to tap Dillard's phone anymore. But he refused to turn over the tapes on the grounds that if he did he would be setting a precedent for future Presidents who would have to turn over *their* tapes to *their* brothers."

I asked Professor Clemente, "Do you think President Nixon was relying on the President Fillmore-Dillard decision when he authorized the tapping of his brother's phone?"

"Either that or the Ulysses S. Grant case.

"If you recall, President Grant was worried about his brother's drinking problems and ordered a tap on his phone. As soon as he got enough evidence on him, Grant ordered his brother arrested for drunkenness. But the case was thrown out when it was revealed that Grant had members of the White House staff break into his brother's doctor's office to steal his brother's files."

Professor Clemente did not think the American public would be alarmed over the news that President Nixon had tapped his brother's phone. "Anyone who has a brother would like to do the same thing."

A NEW JOB FOR GRAY

Rumor has it in Washington that the White House was not very pleased with acting FBI Director L. Patrick Gray's testimony before the Senate Judiciary Committee. There was very serious talk in Washington that the President was about to jettison him. This could have caused great embarrassment to the administration, but trying to keep him as the head of the FBI could have caused even more.

How would they dump him? This is one scenario.

"Mr. Gray, the President wanted me to tell you how

pleased he was with the way you handled yourself during the Senate hearings."

"Thank you, Mr. Haldeman. It's been a tough two weeks, but I got through it."

"I want you to know the President wasn't the least disturbed when you offered to show the Senators on the committee all the raw files on the Watergate bugging investigation."

"I tried to be as forthright as I could, Mr. Haldeman. I felt the Senate had a right to know everything the White House knew about the case."

"Well said, Gray. The director of the FBI must put candor above everything else. You not only told them what they wanted to know, you told them a great deal more, and Mr. Nixon admires that in a man. No President wants someone working for him who keeps secrets from the public."

"That's nice of him to say. I heard there were some people in the White House who were disturbed by my testimony."

"Perish the thought, Gray. We all feel you've done a bang-up job. We'd rather have you admit that we had first crack at all the FBI files than have it come out in Jack Anderson's column in a distorted way. The President was just saying to me the other day, 'I wish all the people in my administration would be as frank and honest with Congress as L. Patrick Gray.' "

"You mean he wasn't mad because I called John Dean III, the White House counsel, a liar?"

"How could the President be mad about that? If someone in the President's family is lying to the FBI, the President wants to *read* about it. How else could he run an honest administration?"

"Well, I think it's good to get all those things out in the open. I wanted to make sure the country would know the FBI would have the same independence under me that it had under J. Edgar Hoover. It would be terrible if they thought I was just another political hack who owed his job to the White House."

"You certainly made *that* point clear with the Senate committee. Say, you never told us you were a naval officer."

"Yes, sir. I served in the Navy for twenty years."

"The President was very pleased to hear that. Gray, we have a job for you that is one of the most important in the world today."

"As director of the FBI I'm at your service."

"This job has nothing to do with the FBI."

"Nothing to do with the FBI?"

"The President wants to put you in charge of clearing all the mines out of Haiphong Harbor. We've checked out thousands of people, and you're the only naval officer we know who can do it."

"But what about the FBI?"

"Anybody can be the head of the FBI, Gray, but how many men can the President trust to sweep the mines out of North Vietnam? Will you do it?"

"I . . . I . . . I don't know."

"Good, here's your ticket to Hanoi. Air Force One is leaving in one hour."

"But . . . but what about my Senate confirmation?"

"You don't have to have Senate confirmation to work on a U.S. minesweeper in Haiphong. In fact, anyone who sweeps mines for the President is entitled to full executive privilege."

THE PRESIDENT BLEW IT

John Ehrlichman testified before the Senate Watergate committee that it was "well within both the constitutional duty and the obligation of the President" for White House aides to break into the office of Dr. Daniel Ellsberg's former psychiatrist.

Senator Sam Ervin, Jr., of North Carolina disputed this interpretation of the President's power and argued there was nothing in the law which gives the President the right to suspend the Fourth Amendment's protection against unreasonable searches and seizures.

Since this is a great constitutional issue, I sought out my old law professor, Heinrich Applebaum, who holds the Chair of Jurisprudence at the Watergate Technical Institute of Perjury.

"Professor, who is right in the constitutional dispute between Senator Ervin and John Ehrlichman?"

"They're both right, and they're both wrong."

"What kind of answer is that?"

"Well, Ehrlichman is right in saying the President of the United States has the duty and obligation to break into anybody's psychiatrist's office that he wants to. But he's wrong in saying that White House aides could do it for the President."

"Do you mean if the President wanted Ellsberg's psychiatric records, he had to break into the office himself?"

"That is correct. He had to perform the burglary personally. Otherwise it would be considered illegal."

"But isn't that kind of hard for a President to do?"

"The writers of your Constitution didn't want to make it easy. They knew that every President of the United States at one time or another would have a desire to break into a psychiatrist's office.

"It's something that no man in power can resist. So they provided that the act itself had to be committed *only* by the President. The writers of the Constitution assumed that this would keep most Presidents from using the power unless it was absolutely necessary.

"Now, had President Nixon borrowed a wig and a camera and tools from the CIA and gone to Dr. Fielding's Beverly Hills office, broken into the files and retrieved the Ellsberg records, he would be acting within the law. But the fact that the President turned over the mission to two White House plumbers was his undoing. As a lawyer he should have known that."

"John Ehrlichman's lawyer, John Wilson, has argued that the President has a vast reservoir of power given to him by Congress which makes it possible for the President to commit what would otherwise be an unlawful act for national security," I said. "Do you agree with this?"

"I certainly do. When it comes to national security, the President can mug, steal and commit arson as long as he is protecting American citizens."

"How do you arrive at that?"

"Because, as Ehrlichman's lawyer has so well pointed out, the courts have never ruled that he *couldn't* do it. Now the President cannot commit these unlawful acts willy-nilly. He has to prove that in some way they have to do with a threat from a foreign power."

"How can he prove it?"

"In the case of Ellsberg's psychiatrist, it's quite possible that Dr. Fielding had made studies of Freud."

"But Freud isn't a foreign power."

"Aha, but where did Freud practice?"

"In Vienna."

"That's all the President needs to justify the break-in."

"Then if I hear you right, Dr. Applebaum, Nixon's only error in the Ellsberg affair is that he did not burglarize the office himself."

"That's the only constitutional issue they've got him on. In fairness to Nixon, though, any President could have made the same mistake."

IV. "ALICE IN WASHINGTON"

MY SON-IN-LAW, THE REPORTER

David Eisenhower once revealed that he might want to pursue a career as a newspaperman and do investigative reporting.

I don't know how David's father-in-law, President Nixon, greeted this news, but it still is no crime to imagine what happened.

"Sir," says David, "I just got my first job as a reporter."

"That's wonderful," the President says. "Some of my best friends are newspapermen."

David says, "It's with the Washington *Post*."

The President gulps on his meat loaf. "The Washington *Post*?"

"Isn't it wonderful?" Julie Nixon Eisenhower says. "That means we can live right here in town. And we can see you when you have to come to Washington on business."

"What sort of job do you have with the Washington *Post*?" the President asks.

"They've made me an investigative reporter, and my first

story is to find out what really went on with the Committee for the Re-Election of the President.''

Julie says, "The *Post* told David if he comes up with anything good, they'll give him a by-line.''

"They want me to see Maurice Stans and ask him what he did with all the cash he collected before April 7,'' David says.

"I wish you wouldn't bother your Uncle Maurice,'' President Nixon says. "He's an awfully busy man.''

"I spoke to him at last Sunday's prayer meeting, and he said he really didn't have anything to do except to talk to his lawyers. He said he'd help me in any way he could.''

"David,'' the President asks, "are you sure this is really what you want to do in life? Investigative reporting is hard work, requiring long hours, and it doesn't pay very well. Now I promised when you married Julie that I wouldn't interfere in your future, but I didn't know you were thinking of becoming a newspaperman.''

Julie says defensively, "David will make a wonderful newspaperman. He's already spoken to Gordon Liddy, Charles Colson and Dwight Chapin, and they've told him some fantastic things about the Committee for the Re-Election of the President. David might even win a Pulitzer Prize when his story comes out.''

"David, when you talked to these people, did you tell them you were working for the Washington *Post*?'' the President asks.

"Of course not. The *Post* told me the very best way to get a story is not to tell your sources who you're working for. This thing is really interesting, Dad. It takes in Mexican bank accounts, ex-CIA employees, bugging equipment, FBI files—''

"I know what it takes in,'' the President says angrily. "But it also involves people in my administration, and it could easily embarrass me.''

"Don't worry, Dad,'' David says. "I checked into that with Ron Ziegler, and he assured me no one in the White House had anything to do with any of the committee's nefarious dealings. You have nothing to worry about.''

"David,'' the President says, "I'm not worried about myself. I'm worried about you and also Julie. Suppose they call you in front of a grand jury and demand that you reveal your sources?''

"I'll refuse—and go to jail," David says.

"Do you realize," Mr. Nixon says, "that would make me the first President in history to have a convict for a son-in-law?"

"Oh, Daddy," says Julie. "You're ruining everything. David is a natural reporter, and the Washington *Post* has great faith in him. Don't spoil everything when we're both so happy."

"All right," the President says. "I don't know what your grandfather would say about this, but I'll give you my blessing."

Julie hugs her father, and David shakes his hand. "But," says the President, "I have one favor to ask of you."

"What's that?" David asks.

"Don't tell your Uncle Spiro what you're doing. He takes these things to heart."

THERE IS A CONSPIRACY

The people who work in the White House are convinced that there is a concerted conspiracy by the media to get Richard Nixon. Until now it has just been conjecture that this conspiracy was well organized and financed by the press and TV networks. But it was hard to prove.

The big break for the White House came when Eberhardt Shroeder, a reporter with the *Daily Gemstone,* was arrested for not revealing his sources in a piece he did on the improvements on King Timahoe's doghouse in San Clemente. Rather than to go to jail, Eberhardt agreed to turn state's evidence and reveal the truth about the media organization which has pledged itself to get the President.

This is a p artial text of Eberhardt's confession:

DA: Who is Mr. Big in the organization?

EBERHARDT: Walter Cronkite. Every newspaperman and TV reporter and commentator reports to him.

DA: How does the conspiracy operate?

EBERHARDT: There are cells all over the country. There is the White House Press Corps Cell, the Camp David Cell, the Key Biscayne Cell and the San Clemente Cell. Cronkite's orders are dispatched to us every morning by Telex. He might assign Joe Alsop to call for Nixon's resignation, or he might order Tom Wicker to do a favorable piece on Archibald Cox, or he could order Bill Buckley to write a column on the President's lack of credibility.

DA: Cronkite does this all alone?

EBERHARDT: No, he has a staff. John Chancellor and Howard K. Smith are in charge of plotting against Nixon for television. Hugh Sidey of *Time* magazine handles all periodicals. Evans and Novak pass on assignments to the columnists. And there is a special cell of editorial writers from the Washington *Post,* New York *Times* and Detroit *Daily News* who make sure the anti-Nixon line is adhered to in editorials.

DA: Who puts up the money for the conspiracy?

EBERHARDT: Walter Cronkite pays for most of it out of his own pocket. Our newspapers and television stations might chip in if we have to fly to Key Biscayne and get the goods on Bebe Rebozo or to L.A. to find out what gives at San Clemente. We also get financing from the Ford Foundation, the Brookings Institute and Masters and Johnson.

DA: How did you use Watergate to embarrass Nixon?

EBERHARDT: We made the whole thing up. There is no James McCord, Jeb Magruder, John Mitchell, Maurice Stans or G. Gordon Liddy. We concocted the whole thing.

DA: Including the resignation of Spiro Agnew?

EBERHARDT: Yup. We take full credit for that one.

DA: Why Agnew? He had nothing to do with Watergate.

EBERHARDT: I guess we just got carried away.

DA: What about the President's tapes?

EBERHARDT: We made that up, too. It really threw the White House for a loop. We didn't know they had any tapes at the time. But it turned out they did. When they revealed that some tapes were missing, they played right into our hands. It was quite a coup for us. Cronkite sent out a "well done" telegram to everyone.

DA: It's obvious you people are well organized.

EBERHARDT: We have to be if we're going to be members of the press—any breakdown in discipline and the White House could get the upper hand.

DA: Suppose a newspaperman or TV commentator won't play ball?

EBERHARDT: Cronkite puts out a contract on him. We bring in reporters from the Chicago newspapers and take the guy for a ride along the Potomac River. It's all very neat and clean.

DA: Well thank you very much. This documents what the White House has been saying all along.

EBERHARDT: Hey, what about me? Now that I've blown the whistle on the conspiracy my life isn't worth yesterday's *Wall Street Journal.*

DA: Don't worry, we'll give you twenty-four-hour protection and find a job for you.

EBERHARDT: Doing what?

DA: How would you like to be a Nixon speechwriter?

TO TELL THE TRUTH

Ladies and gentlemen, welcome to *To Tell the Truth.*

"Number one, what is your name, please?"

"My name is Richard Milhous Nixon."

"Number two, what is your name, please?"

"My name is Richard Milhous Nixon."

"Number three, what is your name, please?"

"My name is Richard Milhous Nixon."

"All right, panel. Now I will read the story. 'I, Richard Milhous Nixon, am the thirty-seventh President of the United States. I was reelected with one of the largest mandates in American history. After my reelection it was revealed that some of my closest aides were involved in dirty tricks, election fraud, breaking and entering and perjury. Congress is now discussing my impeachment.' (Applause.)

"Now, panel, only one of these three contestants is the real Richard Milhous Nixon.

"Let's start the questioning with Kitty."

"Number one, if someone came to you and told you that they wanted to pay hush money to defendants caught in a Watergate break-in, what would you do?"

"I would tell them it was wrong."

"All right, Orson, you're next."

"Number three, it is revealed that on your income tax return you claimed a deduction of five hundred and fifty thousand dollars for donating your Vice Presidential papers to the National Archives. But it turns out the donation was made after the law was changed. What would you say to the charges?"

"I would say that Lyndon B. Johnson made me do it."

"Number one?"

"I would say that I only did what John Kenneth Galbraith has been doing for years."

"Bill?"

"Number one, the House Judiciary Committee has asked for tapes and documents to help them in their impeachment hearings. How would you handle that?"

"First, I would tell the American people that I am willing to cooperate in any way to bring the Watergate matter to a resolution. Then I would tell my lawyer not to turn over any tapes or documents that he considered would in any way hurt the Presidency of the United States."

"Number three?"

"I would say the House is on a fishing expedition, and I am against fishing expeditions of any kind."

"Number two?"

"I would get Ron Ziegler to call it a cheap shot."

"Peggy?"

"Number three, at one press conference you said, John Dean did not tell you about the hush money being paid to the Watergate defendants. At another you admitted he did. How would you square the two statements with the American people?"

"I would say that people will read different things into what I said. But I'm the only one who knows what I meant."

"Number two?"

"I would call in Senator Hugh Scott and show him new evidence that Dean is a liar."

"Number one?"

"I would announce the end of the oil embargo in the Middle East."

"All right, panel, our time is up. Please vote for the person you think is the real Richard Milhous Nixon.

"Now will the real Richard Milhous Nixon please stand . . . I said will the real Richard Milhous Nixon please stand up? Come on, one of you is the real one. Hurry up, we're running out of time. There seems to be a mixup, ladies and gentlemen. No one wants to admit he's the real Nixon.

"Number one, who are you?"

"I am Sarah McClendon, a newspaperwoman."

"Number two, who are you?"

"I am Spiro Agnew, a fiction writer."

"Number three, who are you?"

"I am not a crook."

"ALICE IN WASHINGTON"

Alice was walking down Pennsylvania Avenue when the March Hare asked her, "How would you like to go to a White House press briefing?"

"What's a White House press briefing?" Alice asked.

"That is where they deny what they have already told you, which is the only reason it could be true," the March Hare said.

"It sounds like fun," Alice said.

The March Hare brought Alice into the press room. A chess pawn was standing at a podium.

"Who is that?" Alice asked.

"That is the press secretary. He talks in riddles. Listen."

"Why are transcripts better than tapes?" the press secretary asked.

"I don't know the answer to that one," Alice said to the March Hare. "Why are transcripts better than tapes?" she shouted to everyone's surprise.

The press secretary looked at her with cold blue eyes. "I refuse to comment on that."

Alice looked confused. "Why did he ask us a riddle if he can't give an answer to it?"

The March Hare said, "They don't tell him the answers; they just give him the riddles."

"What a stupid thing," Alice said. "Why is everyone writing in his notebook?"

"They write down everything he says even though they don't believe him."

"Why don't they believe him?" Alice asked.

"Because he makes things up. He has to or there would be no reason to have a briefing."

The press secretary spoke again. "All the evidence is in and it proves beyond a reasonable doubt that the king is innocent of all crimes, ergo, ergo, ergo, et cetera."

"But what about the evidence the king refuses to turn over to the committee?" a dormouse asked.

"That is not evidence," the press secretary replied. "If there was further evidence to prove the king guilty, he would have gladly given it to the committee. The fact that he hasn't turned it over means regretfully there is none. It's as simple as that."

"It doesn't sound very simple to me," Alice said.

"Why can't we hear all the tapes," the Mock Turtle asked, "so we can decide for ourselves who is innocent and who is guilty?"

The press secretary replied, "If you heard the tapes it would only prove the innocent are guilty and the guilty are innocent, and it would serve no purpose but to confuse you. Besides, what you would hear is not what you have read and what you have read is not what you would hear, so it's better not to hear what cannot be read. Isn't that perfectly clear?"

"I feel I'm back at the Mad Hatter's tea party," Alice said.

"Now I will give you some important news today," the press secretary said. "This is on the record. 'Twas brillig, and the slithy toves/Did gyre and gimble in the wabe;/All mimsy were the borogoves,/and the mome raths outgrabe."

Everyone wrote it down.

"What did he say?" Alice asked.

"Nothing," the March Hare replied. "He's just stalling until he can go to lunch."

WHITE HOUSE DENIAL

I was walking past the White House one night when I heard this voice.

"Damn media."

"Who's speaking?" I asked in fright.

"I'm speaking," said the voice. "I'm the White House."

"Don't kid me," I said. "Buildings can't talk."

"Oh, yeah," the voice said. "Then why do you people keep writing, 'The White House said today it wasn't going to hand over any more tapes,' or, 'The White House denied accepting any Howard Hughes money to finance the election'?"

"That's just a figure of speech," I said. "Everyone knows we're not talking about the *White House*—we're talking about the people in it."

"It's easy for you to say that. But if you were sitting where I'm sitting, you wouldn't think it was funny. I haven't done anything. I'm clean as a hound's tooth, and everyone lays everything on me. Houses have feelings, too."

"This is ridiculous," I told the White House. "No one is blaming you for anything that went on there. As far as most people are concerned, you're a pillar of the community."

"Maybe," the voice replied, "but the other night I heard Dan Rather say on television that the White House planned to stonewall the House Judiciary Committee. I've never stonewalled anyone in my life.

"Then John Chancellor said the White House decided to hang tough against special prosecutor Jaworski. How can a house hang tough?"

"I see what you mean."

"I've had a lot of people live in me; some have been good, and some have been bad; but it says right in the lease I am not responsible for anything they do. All I'm supposed to do is provide shelter from the elements and keep up a good façade. Now everyone is throwing stones at me."

"It does seem unfair that the media has played loose with you," I said, "but I'm certain it was just an oversight."

The voice was trembling. "I can understand it when they talk about the Pentagon. That's a *bad* building. When they say the Pentagon asked for a hundred billion dollars, naturally people are going to get sore. Or when the Pentagon admits to an overrun on a nuclear aircraft carrier. But I've never done anything like that. All I've ever done is hold receptions, entertain tourists and pose for pictures. Why don't the media ever write about that?"

"I guess it's your location," I said. "You're an easy target for every reporter in this town."

"Well, I'm staying here," the voice said, "even if what's-his-name gets impeached. Good gravy, just the other day I saw a headline in a newspaper which said WHITE HOUSE ANNOUNCES NEW RISE IN COST OF LIVING. I did no such thing. Why would I be stupid enough to announce something like that?"

"Look, I'm busy," I said. "What do you want from me?"

"I thought you could use a column," he said chortling. "Take any one on the front porch you want."

"Very funny," I said, "but I've been sucked in by the White House one too many times."

"There," cried the voice, "even you're doing it."

"I'm sorry," I said, "but don't forget one thing. When you became the White House, we never promised you a Rose Garden."

UNNAMED SOURCES

One of the big problems a newspaperman in this city has is when he speaks to one unnamed source who contradicts what another unnamed source has told him.

Recently all of us struggled with the dilemma. An unnamed source told the Washington *Post* that a Vice President of the United States was going to resign. Another unnamed source, when contacted, denied it. The big question was who was telling the truth.

The first thing that we had to find out was whether the *Post*'s source was a *reliable* unnamed source. Since we didn't know the unnamed source's name, this was very difficult to do.

There was speculation among many unnamed people in Washington that the unnamed source the Washington *Post* quoted about the Vice President's resignation came from an unmarked building at 1600 Pennsylvania Ave. If it did, that could give it some authenticity. At the same time, so many unnamed sources in this building have been caught in out-and-out lies that the very fact that it originated there might force many of us to discount it.

A source close to the Oval Office denied the unnamed source worked there or at San Clemente. But an unnamed intimate of the Vice President said he strongly suspected that the story was planted with the *Post* to force the VP to resign.

When I had discussed this information with an official high in government circles who asked not to be quoted, he said that the Vice President in question had discussed resignation with many Republican officials whose names he could not give. The consensus was that while he had discussed resignation with some unnamed sources, he had also discussed remaining in office with others. Therefore, it's quite possible that the source that the Washington *Post* talked to was telling the truth as far as he knew it.

Anonymous supporters of a former Texas governor who just became a Republican denied that their people were behind the story. "Our man has no desire to be Vice President of the United States," a highly reliable Houston official leaked to me, "and certainly he would keep any of his sources from talking to the press at this time."

A check at the Justice Department revealed that while unnamed Justice Department officials were going ahead with pursuing the charges made against the Vice President, they had no knowledge of the Vice President's future political plans. A highly placed source close to an unidentified Attorney General who formerly was Secretary of HEW and Defense denied that any leaks about the resignation came from the Justice Department. "We are not the only people in Washington who have unnamed sources."

To make things more confusing, the Washington *Post* referred to its unnamed source as a "Republican Party leader." Since the Republican Party has no leaders, the feeling among a number of unnamed newspapermen here is that this was a smoke screen to protect the *Post*'s real source who probably insisted that his identity be disguised.

Whatever the turth of the matter, there is general agreement here that there are many unnamed sources in Washington who are out to get the Vice President.

At one time the VP thought they were all in the press. But lately he's realized most of the unnamed sources are members of his own political party. He also has reason to believe that the administration is either encouraging the unnamed sources to speak out or at least doing nothing to keep these sources quiet.

Proof of this is that every time someone asks an anonymous White House spokesman where an unnamed President of the United States stands on the Vice President, the spokesman says, not for attribution, "No comment."

QUESTIONS AND ANSWERS

The mail was very heavy from readers some time back, and I felt obligated to answer some of the questions that kept popping up in my letters.

Q. Do you think President Nixon was wrong in turning over only seven of the nine tapes he promised to Judge Sirica?

A. No, I don't. Nobody's perfect and, while the media have been very critical of the President's failure to produce the two missing tapes, no one has given him credit for the seven he turned over. I think we should emphasize the good things the President has been doing and not the bad things.

Q. Why did the President fire special prosecutor Archibald Cox?

A. Because Cox wouldn't stop wearing bow ties. The President hates bow ties, and on several occasions he asked Cox to wear a regular tie like everyone else in the administration. Cox refused, and Nixon had no choice but to get rid of him. It's impossible for a President to run a country when his own special prosecutor refuses to obey a direct order concerning his neckwear.

Q. Why does the President go to Camp David every night?

A. Because he can't get any sleep at the White House. People stand in front of 1600 Pennsylvania Avenue with signs saying HONK IF YOU THINK NIXON SHOULD BE IMPEACHED, and the noise is deafening. The best solution would be if they held up signs saying HONK IF YOU BELIEVE HIM. Then Washington would become the quietest city in the country.

Q. Who are the 27 percent of the American people in the Gallup Poll who still think Nixon is doing a good job as President?

A. Julie and David Eisenhower, Tricia Cox, Bebe Rebozo, Robert Abplanalp, General Alexander Haig, Ron Ziegler and the entire board of directors of ITT.

Q. Why are the press and TV so mean to Nixon?

A. They've been mad at him ever since 1962 when he told them they would not have Nixon to kick around anymore. The press never forgets, and everything you've been reading about Watergate is nothing but the media's way of proving they can kick Nixon around any time they want to.

Q. Who was Spiro Agnew?

A. He was a former Vice President of the United States who served during the Nixon administration until he got into some difficulty over his income taxes. While he has been completely forgotten, a few old-timers remember him as being rather tall and a neat dresser.

Q. The Constitution provides that a President can be impeached for high crimes and misdemeanors. What are they?

A. A high crime would be accepting a large political contribution from the milk producers in exchange for raising the price of milk. A misdemeanor could be impounding funds so schoolchildren could not get any of this milk free.

Q. Has Nixon's personal enemy list gotten any longer since his recent troubles?

A. Would you believe the Washington, Maryland and Virginia telephone books?

Q. If the President resigns, how much of the $10,000,000

he spent on improving his homes in San Clemente and Key Biscayne will be returned to the government?

A. According to his accountants, about $34.75.

Q. No President has been under so much criticism and pressure in history. Is Nixon hurting because of it?

A. Only when he laughs.

A GREAT MOVIE BY FLETCH

It's getting harder and harder to sell fiction to the movies these days. The other day a friend of mine went in to see the producers at Magna Cum Laude Productions.

"Hi, Fletch. What have you got for us this time?"

"I think I've got a fantastic yarn. It concerns a President of the United States at some time in the future."

"Go ahead, Fletch. Your President stories are always good."

"Well, you see there is this President, and he's up for reelection, and his party has to raise fifteen million dollars because the opposition party has a chance of beating him. So a committee is set up to collect the money and spend it. Now this committee decides to allocate a large sum of money for dirty tricks, sabotage, bugging and that sort of stuff."

"It's pretty farfetched so far, Fletch, but go ahead."

"The White House hires a former FBI agent and a former CIA agent—"

"Wait a minute, Fletch. Did you say the *White House* hires them?"

"Right. They're paid by the committee, but they work right in the White House. Their jobs are to get the goods on the opposition by bugging, forgery and burglary."

"In the script, Fletch, does the President know about all this?"

"We don't find out until later. That's where the suspense comes in. Anyhow, the dirty tricks team made up of Cubans—"

"Hold it, Fletch. Did you say Cubans?"

"Right, the Cubans think they're working to overthrow Castro. Anyway they try to plant a bug in the opposition party's headquarters, but they're caught. Now this is where the picture gets good. The White House is afraid the whole operation will be blown, so they work out a fantastic cover-up with the CIA, the FBI and the Justice Department."

"Good grief, Fletch," a producer says. "You're talking about the White House, the Justice Department, the FBI and the CIA. Do you expect the public to buy all that?"

"It gets better," Fletch says. "One of the guys, an ex-CIA man, talks and implicates the former Attorney General of the United States."

"Holy smoke," a producer says. "What have you been drinking?"

"Then," continues Fletch, "the thing really unravels. Everyone on the committee is out to save his own skin, and they implicate the President's own legal counsel and half the White House staff, including his two highest aides. The President goes on the air and says he is going to get to the bottom of the cover-up no matter where it leads. He fires his Attorney General and appoints the Secretary of Defense to head up the investigation."

"Thanks a lot, Fletch," a producer says. "Don't call us, we'll call you."

"Wait," cries Fletch, "I'm not finished. The White House legal counsel not only confesses to the whole thing but says the President knew about it all along."

"You have two minutes, Fletch."

"The President then goes on nationwide television and says that he has just received startling new information that he is involved in the whole affair and because of this new development, he is going to resign. The picture ends with the Vice President taking the oath of office and Frank Sinatra singing 'God Bless America.'"

There is dead silence in the room.

Finally, one of the producers speaks. "Get the hell out of here, Fletch. And if you ever bring us a cockamamie script like this again, we'll ban you from the studio for life."

THE FBI AND THE WATERGATE

As a big fan of *The FBI* television show, I am waiting with bated breath for them to dramatize the role the FBI played in the Watergate bugging case. The script should go something like this:

ACT 1
Opening shot of Watergate. Voice-over: "In the early hours of June 17, 1972, five men broke into Democratic National Committee headquarters at the Watergate while two accomplices waited nervously across the street in the Howard Johnson Motel. All seven were arrested. The next morning at eight thirty Special Agent Lewis Erskine [played by Efrem Zimbalist Jr.] is called in by his superior, Arthur Ward.

"Erskine, this is one of the toughest cases the FBI has ever had to work on. We have to find out who was behind the bugging of the Democratic National Committee headquarters at the Watergate. If these mad fiends are allowed to continue their wiretapping, it could destroy the United States of America forever."

"I'll get right on it."

"We can't leave a stone unturned in rooting out these vicious criminal rats who would do anything to sabotage one of the major political parties in the country. Do you understand?"

"We'll get them, sir."

ACT 2
Erskine and his assistant, Tom Colby, are questioning members of the Committee for the Re-Election of the President. A man is sitting there taking notes.

"Who are you?" Erskine asks.

"I'm just sitting in to make sure they don't say anything that might reflect on the committee."

"Get out of here," Colby orders.

The man answers, "I have this letter from the White House

which says I can be present whenever one of our people is interrogated."

Erskine reads the letter. It's signed by Dwight Chapin, the President's appointments secretary.

He turns to Colby. "Something is fishy here. We'd better talk to Chapin."

"You can't talk to Chapin unless John Dean, the President's legal counsel, is present," the man says.

"What's Dean got to do with this?"

"He's in charge of the President's investigation of the Watergate bugging."

"Well, we'd better talk to Dean then."

"You can't talk to Dean unless you get permission from H. R. Haldeman, the President's special assistant."

"Then we'll talk to Haldeman."

"You can't talk to Haldeman unless you speak to the acting director of the FBI, L. Patrick Gray."

"Wow," says Erskine, "this really is a tough case."

ACT 3

Erskine reports to his superior, Arthur Ward. "We think we have very interesting information. The Watergate case was part of a larger plan by the Committee for the Re-Election of the President to sabotage the Democrats. Hundreds of thousands of dollars in cash was raised by Maurice Stans, given to Hugh Sloan, Jr., the treasurer, and dispensed through Herbert W. Kalmbach, the President's personal lawyer. The money was given to a Gordon Liddy and a Donald Segretti. The White House seems to be in this up to its ears."

"Good," says Ward. "Type up a copy of the report and send it to the White House immediately."

"But they're involved."

"Exactly. And for that reason they should know what we've got on them."

"But we've never given our files to people involved in a crime before."

"Erskine, you've got a good future with the bureau. Don't louse it up by getting the acting director mad at you."

"I have to worry about my image. I want to speak to the acting director about this personally."

"You can't, Erskine."

"Why not?"

"He's in Ohio making a nonpolitical speech for Mr.
Nixon."

THEY STOLE MY STUFF

The paranoia in Washington gets worse and worse. Even I
started feeling it, and I went to see a psychiatrist.

"What seems to be the problem?" he asked.

"Everyone is stealing my stuff," I said in anguish.

"Can you be more specific?" he asked.

"Well, you see a couple of years ago things were very dull
in Washington, and there wasn't much to write about except
impoundment and the SALT talks. So I decided to do
something to jazz up the column. One day I was walking by
the Watergate and I thought to myself, 'Wouldn't it be a gas if
the Republicans bugged the headquarters of the Democratic
Party?'"

"When did you think of this?"

"Sometime in June of 1972. I thought it would make a very
funny column. At first I decided to have one man bug the
Democrats, but then I got worried that some people might
take me seriously, so I decided to make it seven. It seemed
more outrageous to have seven people get involved in
something that stupid."

"No one in his right mind would have believed it," the
psychiatrist agreed.

"Well, the column was a big hit, so I decided to follow it up
with another funny column about the Committee to Re-Elect
the President being involved in the break-in, including the
former Attorney General of the United States."

"I recall the piece. It was very amusing, particularly the
part about all the money that was spent on the campaign," the
psychiatrist said.

"Well, you can't imagine the success of this column. It was

so different from anything coming out of Washington. So I did a follow-up column where I just let my imagination go wild. I traced the break-in to the White House. I invented several characters whom I called H. R. Haldeman, John Ehrlichman, John Dean and Charles Colson. I decided it would be very funny if one of the characters, John Dean, blew the whistle on the President of the United States."

"Weren't you afraid some people would believe you?" the psychiatrist asked.

"There is always the danger when you're writing satire that a few people will take you seriously. But since I was talking about the President, I was certain no one in his right mind would accept the tale as anything but pure fiction. Anyone with any brains would have to know the whole thing was a big put-on. Frankly I wanted to stop the gag right there, but I had so many requests for further installments that I had no choice but to continue the series.

"I was really stuck as to how to make the thing even more outlandish until one day I was fooling around with my daughter's tape machine and suddenly I got the wildest idea of all. I decided to write that the President had taped *all* his conversations in the White House and that these tapes would implicate him in the Watergate scandal. I said with tongue in cheek, or course, that the evidence would lead to his impeachment."

"I remember that column," said the psychiatrist, "and frankly I thought you had gone too far."

"Well," I said defensively, "*some* people thought it was funny."

"All right then," the psychiatrist said. "What seems to be the problem?"

"Just this. Everyone is stealing my story. Like an idiot I never copyrighted it, and now every time you pick up a paper or turn on the TV they're using my characters and plot. I invented all those people. THEY BELONG TO ME. WATERGATE NEVER HAPPENED EXCEPT IN MY MIND. DOCTOR, YOU HAVE TO HELP ME."

"Here's a prescription for some Valium. We'll talk more about it next week."

GOOD NEWS AND BAD NEWS

In a speech in Huntsville, Alabama, on "Honor America Day" President Nixon said, "In the nation's capital there is a tendency for partisanship to take over from statesmanship. In the nation's capital sometimes there is a tendency in the reporting of the news—I do not say this critically, it's simply a fact of life—that bad news is news and good news is not news."

I couldn't agree with the President more.

But in fairness to the people reporting the news, the problem is not one of reporting bad news or good news but of knowing what is good news as opposed to bad news. When you work in Washington, it's difficult to distinguish the difference, and what may sound like bad news to President Nixon is actually good news to somebody else.

For example, there was a special election in Grand Rapids, Michigan, for Vice President Jerry Ford's Congressional seat, and for the first time in sixty-four years a Democrat won. Now this was obviously bad news for the President, but it was good news for the Democrats. Had the press not reported this, they wouldn't know if they were suppressing good news or bad news.

Another example of the cloudy issue of good news and bad news is former Vice President Agnew's Secret Service detail. When the press played up the fact that Mr. Agnew still had Secret Service protection and had taken a flock of them to Palm Springs to stay with Frank Sinatra, this was bad news for the administration. But when the stories forced the White House to take the Secret Service away from Mr. Agnew, this was good news for the American taxpayer. Had the press not printed the bad news, there would have never been any good news to follow up with. The Agnew case proved that the revelation of bad news can have a good effect.

Every day the Washington press corps wrestles with some great moral dilemma. Take the case of the Watergate tapes. When the President decided to turn over the nine tapes to the special prosecutor, that was good news. But when he discovered that two of nine did not exist, that was bad news. In this case the President had a right to be angry. Instead of talking about the seven he turned over to the special prosecutor, the press made an issue of the two that were missing. Then, to complicate matters, it was discovered that 18½ minutes of one tape had been erased. This was bad news. But what the media failed to report was the good news which was that except for the 18½ -minute gap, the rest of the tape was clear as a bell.

Even administration officials have a hard time sorting out good news from bad news. Recently Roy Ash, the head of the Office of Management and Budget, said the energy crisis was only temporary and would soon be over.

This was good news, and for once the media revealed it. Then William Simon, the energy czar, spoke out and said Ash didn't know what the hell he was talking about and that the energy crisis would be with us for a long time to come. This was bad news, and it really hurt the press to reveal it so soon after Ash's good news.

I think what the President was talking about was the Washington press corps' reluctance to print good news about him. A perfect illustration is that recent polls revealed that the American people held Congress in lower esteem than the President of the United States by five percentage points. Unfortunately, though, the President at the time of the poll was held in high esteem by only 26 percent of the people. So you could say this was either good news for the President or bad news for the country.

It would be most helpful for people in Washington if the government could set up guidelines for us so we could know what good news is. The Kremlin does this for the press in the Soviet Union, and it works like a dream.

FLETCH NEVER GIVES UP

Fletch Knebel never gives up. Recently he was back in Hollywood trying to sell Magna Cum Laude Productions another movie idea.

"All right, Fletch, what is it this time?"

"I've got a crazy idea. It's a spy story."

"We can always use a spy story. What's it about, the Russians or the Chinese?"

"It's more complicated than that. It's about the Pentagon spying on the White House."

"Good grief, Fletch. . . ."

"Hear me out. There's this head of the Joint Chiefs of Staff, an admiral, and he's worried that the White House might do something without him knowing about it."

"Like what?"

"Make a deal with Ghana or Panama or something. I haven't worked that out yet. So, anyway, he expresses his nervousness to two admirals, who set up their own spy ring right in the White House."

"Is this a remake of *Seven Days in May?*"

"No, this is all new stuff. The spy turns out to be a yeoman first class who has access to all the papers in the White House. Every night before he goes home he steals documents from the office of Henry Kay, the President's adviser on foreign affairs. The material is delivered to the Joint Chiefs of Staff in the morning, and they know exactly what the White House is up to."

"Where's the love story?"

"Henry Kay is a secret swinger, and on one of his dates in Egypt, while he's sitting in front of the Pyramids with a Wave lieutenant who works for the admiral, she reveals that she knows what Henry said to Mao Tse-tung on his recent trip to Peking.

"Henry is aware that the only people who know what he said to Mao Tse-tung were Mrs. Mao Tse-tung, President Nixon and Jack Anderson. In a fury he flies back to Washington after stopping off in Israel, Jordan, Liberia, Moscow, New Delhi and South Korea. He reports to the President that the Pentagon has planted a spy in the White House.

"The President orders the Secret Service to tap the telephone of his brother Donald. When this does not produce any information, the President orders the plumbers to follow his son-in-law David Eisenhower for a month.

"When this doesn't produce any results, Henry orders a bug on the telephone of Zsa Zsa Gabor. But despite all these precautions Henry's memos keep showing up on the Joint Chiefs' desks.

"One evening Henry is at a state dinner at the White House, and he notices the Joint Chiefs' admiral wearing a set of cuff links that Henry had thrown away in a burn bag the day before.

"Henry asks the admiral where he got the cuff links.

"The admiral says, 'They were given to me by a very dear golf-playing friend of mine, a yeoman first class, who never forgets my birthday.'

"Henry's no fool, and he puts two and two together. He tells the admiral, 'Your yeoman is a spy.'

"The admiral is shocked. 'I'll have him court-martialed right away.'

"Henry is about to concur when the Wave lieutenant puts her arms around him and says, 'If you love me, you'll forget the whole thing.'

"The movie ends with Henry and the Wave walking hand in hand on a sandy white beach in New Zealand, while the yeoman hiding behind a rock photographs the contents of Henry's briefcase.''

V. GAME PLAN

MIDDLE AMERICA REMEMBERS WATERGATE

Long after Watergate is over, certain phrases repeated during the hearings will remain with us.

Already they are being used by Middle America to cover various situations.

The other day at exactly 2:30 A.M. Mintonburger staggered into the hallway of his house. His tie was askew, there was lipstick on his collar, and there was a strong odor of alcohol on his breath.

Mrs. Mintonburger in her dressing gown was waiting for him. "Do you swear to tell the truth, the whole truth and nothing but the truth, so help you God?"

"Yes, sir."

"Where the hell have you been?"

"I'm sorry. I didn't hear the question."

"I said where the hell have you been?"

"To the best of my recollection I was at Reilly's Bar and Grill."

"Whom were you there with?"

"I don't have all my records with me, but I believe I was there with Sam Carlsberg, Ed Tuborg and Charlie Schlitz."

"What was discussed at the bar until two-thirty in the morning?"

"What meeting are we talking about now?"

"The one you just came from."

"Well, let's see. As far as I recall, we discussed the trade of running-back Duane Thomas to the Washington Redskins."

"Is that all you talked about?"

"To the best of my knowledge I believe that is all we talked about. You must remember, Senator . . . I mean, dear . . . that we're talking about something that happened several hours ago, and although I'm trying to be as candid as possible, it is very difficult for me to remember everything that took place last night."

"All right," Mrs. Mintonburger said, going over some notes she was holding in her hand, "let's go on to another subject. What's that lipstick doing on your collar?"

"I never heard of any lipstick on my collar."

"It's right there."

"I believe we have to put this in the proper context. I recall during the evening brushing past a lady who had been pushed into me by a man. Her lips hit me right on the collar."

"And that is your story?"

"As far as that particular incident is concerned, I would say it is an accurate description of it at that point in time."

"Would it surprise you, Mr. Mintonburger, that I called Reilly's Bar at midnight and spoke to Reilly, and he said you hadn't been in all evening?"

"What night are we talking about now?"

"Tonight."

"I believe Reilly is mistaken. I specifically remember being there."

"Then you would say that Reilly is not telling the truth?"

"On this particular point, I would say he is not."

"Why would Reilly lie about your not being in his bar?"

"To protect himself. Reilly has perjured himself on many occasions, and he is constantly seeking ways of getting immunity."

"Well, let me ask you this. Do you think you have a right coming in drunk at two-thirty in the morning with lipstick on your collar?"

"In hindsight it was probably a bad idea. But at that point in time when I did those things, I was only following the orders of my superiors, Sam Carlsberg, Ed Tuborg and Charlie Schlitz. As I look back on it now, I should have inquired why they were asking me to do certain things, which may under the present atmosphere appear to some to be evidence of wrongdoing."

"One final question, Mr. Mintonburger. What is your advice to other husbands who might find themselves in the same position?"

"Well, sir, I would say that I am not proud of what I did, and I guess I am lacking in moral fiber which caused me to go along with what everybody else was doing."

Mr. Mintonburger, thank you for your candid and forthright testimony. You have been a very cooperative witness. One more thing, will you be available for further questioning tomorrow morning if it is needed?"

"That's why I'm here."

THE CRACKPOT

The United States is having a very difficult time trying to figure out how to celebrate its two hundredth anniversary. Many ideas have been suggested for the bicentennial, but few have grabbed the American people. The President's commission on the anniversary is bogged down in red tape, and no one is certain we will have a celebration at all.

The other day a man walked into my office and said he had a revolutionary plan for Americans to celebrate their country's two hundredth birthday.

I tried to be polite, but it was difficult because I have people like this coming in to see me all the time.

"Make it brief," I said.

"Well," he said hesitatingly, "I have this idea to celebrate two hundred years of independence and it won't cost the country a cent."

"Get to it," I said impatiently.

"Why don't we, in 1976, hold the *first* honest Presidential election in the history of the country?"

"You're out of your mind," I said.

"I've got it worked out here on paper. There would be only one fund-raising committee in each party, and no one would be allowed to contribute more than twenty-five dollars to a Presidential candidate."

"Impossible," I said. "What would happen to your thousand-dollars-a-plate dinners? What about people who want to buy ambassadorships and jobs in the government? How about the oil companies, the airline companies, the labor unions and milk producers? Are you going to be able to keep them from giving more than twenty-five dollars to a Presidential campaign?"

"I know it's a wild idea," the man said, "but it could work. No one would be permitted to give any donations in cash. Every gift would have to be by check or money order. All moneys would have to be accounted for, and if there is any hanky-panky committed by the finance committee of either party, the Presidential candidate of that party would automatically forfeit the election."

"Have you lost your senses?" I said, trying to hold my temper. "Do you know what it costs to run a Presidential campaign? Do you have any idea of the payroll, printing bills, television fees and national security costs that it takes to elect a President of the United States?"

"Well, if it costs too much," the man said, "then let's eliminate a lot of it. Why should money be the decisive factor in electing a President of the United States?"

"Because money is the mother's milk of politics!" I shouted. "Do you think Nixon would be President of the United States today if people were allowed to contribute only twenty-five dollars to his election?"

"I'm not talking about Nixon," the man said. "I'm talking about 1976. Look, I'm not saying we would have to continue with my plan. But I thought for just *one* Presidential election we could do it. And it's not just a ceiling on money that I'm advocating. When I talk about an honest election, I mean the candidates would have to stick to the issues. There would be no name-calling or dirty advertisements or double agents, no bugging or wiretapping or reading other people's mail."

"You've got to be kidding. This country is not ready for an honest Presidential election, and you know it. We've been brought up on the principle that in politics anything goes. Everyone knows the only reason one party resorts to dirty tricks is that if they don't, the other party will. Do you expect us to change our life-style just because we're celebrating our two hundredth anniversary?"

"That's what everyone tells me," he said sadly, and he got up to leave.

After his departure, my secretary asked me what it was all about.

"He's some crackpot who wants to hold an honest Presidential election. They shouldn't allow guys like that to wander around loose."

GAME PLAN

My friend Moonslinger is a skeptic by nature, and one day, as we were having a drink together at the Press Club, he said, "Nixon's credibility has reached a new low. You don't know what to believe anymore."

"I always believe the President of the United States. That's how I was brought up."

"Yeah, but this is different. Every day you read the paper witnesses say Nixon knew more about the Watergate than he did the day before."

"We used to have a saying in France," I told Moonslinger, "*Honi soit qui mal y pense* which means 'Evil to him who thinks evil.'"

"Don't you have it anymore?" Moonslinger asked.

"Not since Pompidou was elected."

"Well, anyway," he persisted, "what worries me is that if we can't believe the President on the Watergate, how can we believe him on Vietnam? For example, how can we be sure that we have Peace with Honor?"

I said angrily, "The President would never lie to us about something like *that.*"

"But suppose, just suppose, there isn't any Peace with Honor there and the South Vietnamese and North Vietnamese are still fighting?"

"Impossible," I said. "After ten long years we have achieved a peace in Indochina that everyone can live with."

"But let's say, just for argument's sake, that something went wrong. Suppose after Kissinger's meeting in Paris with Le Duc Tho, the President goes on the air and says he has just received new information that we don't have Peace with Honor in Vietnam. Will the American people believe him?"

"Of course they will."

"All right, let's go one step further," Moonslinger said. "Suppose he says because of this new information, he will be obligated to start bombing North Vietnam again because he doesn't want to be the first *impeached* President in the history of the United States to lose a war?"

"Then the American people will have to support him, unless, of course, you want Cambodia to fall."

"Nobody wants Cambodia to fall," Moonslinger said. "But because of the President's credibility problem, many Americans may not believe him when he says he has to bomb again. This could bring the students and antidemonstrators out into the streets."

"That's where the President likes them," I said. "He wants his enemies out there in the streets where he can see them."

"Okay, then you have demonstrations, riots, arrests and Jane Fonda. The President declares a national emergency and, whammo, everyone forgets about Watergate."

"Moonslinger, are you trying to tell me the President would bomb North Vietnam to take our minds off a domestic scandal in his own administration?"

"Why not? What has he got to lose?"

"It's too farfetched," I said adamantly.

"Any more farfetched than the White House breaking into Daniel Ellsberg's psychiatrist's office with equipment lent them by the CIA?"

"That's different," I said. "The President had no choice."

"All I can tell you is when Nixon goes on the air in a few weeks and says, 'My fellow Americans,' the North Vietnamese had better head for their bomb shelters."

"Moonslinger," I said, "the trouble with you is that just because of a third-rate burglary at the Watergate, you've lost your faith in the leaders of our land."

THE ELECTION IS OFF

Has the President done all he can do in regards to the Watergate bugging scandal? Some people think he hasn't. One, a Democrat friend of mine named Osgood Timishoe, announced: "The University of Oklahoma forfeited nine football games plus the Sugar Bowl because someone cheated on their players' grades."

"What has that got to do with the Watergate?" I asked.

"I believe Nixon should forfeit the election."

"Have you gone mad, Osgood?" I said in horror. "The President's been in office for too long. He can't just up and forfeit at this late date."

"Why not? Oklahoma played their games the same fall as the elction they forfeited the next spring. The President's the number one football fan in the country, and he should take the lead from the number two college football team."

"But why would he do it?" I asked.

"Because everyone in this country knows that Nixon would never want to win a contest if cheating were involved. He has too much principle for that. The Presidency of the United States isn't worth the price if you have to gain it by deceit. The only honorable thing to do would be for the President to go on national television this week and say, 'Because of startling new information that I have just received concerning the Watergate, I am forfeiting the election to my worthy opponent, Senator George McGovern.'"

"But, Osgood, if the President forfeits the election now, what happens to everything that has already taken place such as Peace with Honor in Vietnam, the dollar devaluation, meat prices, the impounding of funds?"

"They would all be inoperative. The President's forfeiture would be the only thing operative. President McGovern would have to start from scratch, which he's used to doing anyway."

"There must be another solution," I protested. "Perhaps rather than forfeit, the President could ask for a new election with an entirely new team of players on the Committee for the Re-Election of the President."

"Did the University of Oklahoma ask to replay Penn State in the Sugar Bowl?" Osgood asked.

"But that's different," I replied.

"It may be to some people, but I'm not sure it is to Richard M. Nixon. How can he face the public for the next two and a half years knowing he won the election by unfair methods? How can the U.S. Marine band play 'Hail to the Chief' when the Chief's own people in the White House fixed the election so Nixon would be a sure thing?"

"But surely Nixon knows in his heart that he would have won the election with or without the tampering of the Watergate."

"There will always be that question," Osgood said. "It isn't good for the country to have a President who will never be certain that he had a *real* mandate from the people."

"Even if you're right, are you sure George McGovern still wants to be President?"

"I believe so. He's having a lot of trouble in South Dakota running for Senator, so I think he'd accept Nixon's offer."

"Wait a minute," I said, "If Nixon forfeits the Presidency, what does he do for the next two and a half years?"

"He could become the president of the University of Oklahoma."

WATERGATE AND SAUSAGE

Did you know that the price of meat has a direct bearing on the Watergate bugging scandal? I didn't until I saw Helmut Dragonfield at the supermarket the other day.

We were standing in the check-out line, and Helmut said to me, "This Watergate case smells to high heaven. It really boils me that men in high office can lie through their teeth about matters that affect the very fabric of American democracy."

"Helmut," I reminded him, "you didn't seem very excited about the Watergate during the elections."

"That," said my friend, "was because you could still get a decent steak for a dollar fifty."

"Are you trying to tell me the only reason you are appalled at what happened at the Watergate is because the price of steak has gone up?"

"Not only steak," Helmut said. "What about eggs and fish and cheese and fruit and vegetables? Why shouldn't I be mad about what the Republicans did at the Watergate when I'm paying a dollar thirty-five for two pork chops?"

"But, Helmut, why didn't you get mad at the time the crime was committed?"

"Because McGovern was running for President. I didn't want to believe the Nixon people would do such things, because if I did, that meant I would have voted for the Democrats."

"Helmut, if it is a moral issue now, it was a moral issue then. You can't get mad about the Watergate because food prices have gone up."

"Who says I can't? You don't seem to understand much about the American people. As long as the economy is good, wages are high and inflation is in check, they couldn't care less what the Republicans were doing to the Democrats. But now that inflation is running wild, the stock market is at its lowest ebb and the dollar is in so much trouble, we're seeing the Watergate in a new light. Something is rotten in Denmark, and I hope the Senate Investigating Committee gets to the bottom of it."

"I'm glad you feel that way, Helmut. It shows you really care about your country."

"Of course I do. Gas is going up, shoes are going up, booze is going up. When I pay fifty-nine cents for a can of tomatoes, I'm not going to put up with corruption in the White House, too."

"Do you think if food prices went down, the Watergate affair would blow over?"

"I'm certain of it. All Nixon has to do is get bacon down to eighty-five cents a pound, and I'll give his staff the benefit of the doubt on anything they say about their role in the Watergate. But as long as corn is selling for fifty cents a can, I say let the grand jury indict them all."

"I can't think of a better reason for the President to lower food prices," I said.

Helmut pushed his cart up to the counter. As the clerk rang up each item on his cash register, Helmut mumbled, "I want to hear what John Dean III has to say. . . . Why are they hiding Donald Segretti? . . . John Mitchell knows more than he's telling. . . . Maurice Stans, when are you going to tell us the truth? . . . L. Patrick Gray, where were you when we needed you? . . ."

I was terribly embarrassed when it came my turn to pay for my basket of food, and I apologized to the cashier for Helmut's behavior.

"Think nothing of it," the clerk said. "Everyone who comes to my counter has been talking to himself about the Watergate since sausage meat went up to ninety-five cents a pound."

NOT FUN FOR LIBERALS

You would think these would be great times for liberals, but I've discovered many of them are in a deep depression.

Partridge was as glum as I've ever seen him the other day.

"These are lousy times for all of us," he said as he munched on a watercress salad.

"How can you say that, Partridge? You should be rejoicing with Watergate and the fact that Nixon is on the ropes."

"It's no fun being against Nixon anymore. Everyone's against Nixon. Who the hell wants to be in the mainstream of American politics? Who wants to march to somebody else's drum?"

"I don't understand."

"The first four years it was great to be against Nixon. You could scream and shout about what the man was doing to the country, and everyone thought you were some kind of nut. People would argue with you or ignore you.

"But at least you knew that you were in the minority, and you had a warm feeling because you were sure all of them were wrong and you were right.

"I remember going to parties and people insulting me because I called Nixon a crook. I attended anti-Vietnam rallies, and the FBI took my picture. I circulated petitions against Attorney General Mitchell, and I wrote letters to editors against Carswell being appointed to the Supreme Court.

"Maybe I was considered a radical left-winger, but by gum I had an identity of my own. Then Watergate took place, and as time went on, all the people I used to argue with started to come over to my side.

"Whatever I accused Nixon of brought cheers from the crowd. The very people who called me vile names admitted I'd been right all along. When I discovered Nixon had no defenders, something within me died."

"I see what you mean," I said.

"I guess the final blow came when Senator James Buckley asked for the President to resign. Can you imagine how it feels for a dyed-in-the-wool liberal to be on the same side as a Buckley?"

"It doesn't leave you any place to go."

"We liberals," Partridge said, "can only thrive when we're in opposition to somebody, in a hopeless cause. We're not any good when the whole damn country is echoing everything we say.

"I think I'll get out of politics," he said in disgust.

"I would hate to see you do that, Partridge," I told him. "I have an idea that might resolve your problem. As long as the majority of the country is against Nixon, why don't you defend him?"

"You can't be serious," he said.

"Why not? It would put you back in the minority again, and you could find yourself being ostracized by the same people who took issue with you before Watergate. Only this time you would be on Nixon's side, and they would be against him. It would be a great way to get back at Buckley."

"I'll do it," he said excitedly. "Talk about being involved in a hopeless cause. This could top them all."

A BUSHWHACKED TIME MACHINE

Americans are groggy from keeping up with all the things happening to their government. So far the people being blamed for this are the press, overzealous aides in the Nixon administration, the Justice Department and the Senate Watergate committee.

But Teebold Ratameyer, a computer expert, has another theory. He thinks the Time Machine is out of synchronization. He feels that unless someone gets it back in order, we will never be able to sort out our troubles.

"As far as I know," he told me, "the Time Machine was working perfectly up until the election. Nixon received his mandate, and the machine had been programmed to give us a peace with honor soon afterward. But then someone fed Watergate into the machine, and it's been acting erratically ever since."

"How do you mean?"

"Well, for one thing, this is the first time in history that you've had gasoline rationing *after* a war was over. In fact, it was only after we *stopped* fighting that we had shortages of any kind."

"It does sound haywire," I admitted.

"Now look at Watergate. The Time Machine was programmed for a scandal in Nixon's administration . . . every administration must have at least *one*. But Watergate produced a dozen, plus two constitutional crises in one year."

"Two?"

"That's correct. You have the question of the President being forced to give up his tapes, and you have the question of whether a Vice President can be indicted for a crime before he's impeached. In the past, the Time Machine has only given us one constitutional crisis every twenty years."

"Maybe someone has speeded up the machine," I suggested.

"That's a possibility," Ratameyer said. "It might explain the rate of inflation. We know that we must expect a certain amount of inflation every year, but what's been happening in the last six months is ridiculous. Only a Time Machine that's gone completely berserk could allow prices to increase at the rate they have."

"Do you think the Democrats have been messing with the Time Machine to make Nixon look bad?"

"I doubt it," said Ratameyer. "They're just as much victims of it as the Republicans. Here they have the greatest political scandal in the history of the nation, and they don't even know what to do with it. Anyone who could fix a Time Machine would be bright enough to have a plan."

"I must admit your theory has some validity."

"The Time Machine is not only out of whack politically, but it's also out of whack socially. More people are getting divorced than getting married this year."

"That in itself is a constitutional crisis," I said.

"We've gone to the moon, but we can't heat our homes. And the higher the standard of living gets in this country, the more chance you have of choking to death."

"What can we do?"

"Someone has got to get to the Time Machine and repair it. We've got to put it back in working order before it gets to all of us."

"But who could do it?" I asked.

"It's really a job for Superman."

"Why not?"

"I called him," said Ratameyer, "but he told me he doesn't make house calls."

DEMOCRATS FOR EHRLICHMAN

My friend Cotswald, who was a Democrat for Nixon, seemed very depressed when I found him in a bar during the Watergate hearings.

I asked him what the problem was.

"I've been watching the hearings all week," he said, "and it's got me down."

"Don't worry," I said, trying to cheer him up, "it's John Dean's word against the President's. It's still quite possible that Nixon had nothing to do with Watergate or the cover-up."

"That's just the point," Cotswald said. "Suppose Nixon didn't have anything to do with Watergate? The White House defense is that Nixon didn't know anything about anything. The whole country was being run by Haldeman and Ehrlichman. Wouldn't that depress you?"

"Well, it wouldn't make me happy," I admitted.

"I didn't vote for Haldeman and Ehrlichman," Cotswald said bitterly. "I voted for Nixon. If I had known he was going to turn over the Presidency of the country to two flunkies, I sure as hell would have thought twice about it."

"But President Nixon had the final say on all their decisions," I pointed out.

"We don't know that. From what we've heard, Ehrlichman and Haldeman gave orders to the Justice Department, the FBI, the CIA, the State Department and everybody else.

"Everyone in the White House except John Dean says the President had no idea what anybody was doing. If we believe this, it means that Ehrlichman and Haldeman were running the show. This is a frightening thought—much worse than having the President implicated in Watergate."

"But," I protested, "the President can't do everything himself. He has to have aides to carry out his orders."

"Dammit," said Cotswald, "if they carried out the President's orders, it means the President knew what was going on. If they did it on their own, that means I was a Democrat for Haldeman and Ehrlichman. That's a terrible thing for any man to live with."

"But Haldeman and Ehrlichman may have been acting on their own just in regard to Watergate," I said. "The rest of the time they may have been acting on orders from the President."

"How do we know that? All the testimony indicates no one ever got in to see the President. We don't even know if the

President was there half the time. The only thing Nixon read was Pat Buchanan's résumé of the news every morning. Every White House staffer, Cabinet officer and Nixon appointee reported to Haldeman and Ehrlichman. When Haldeman and Ehrlichman gave orders, they said they were speaking for the President. But all the proof so far is that they did anything they darned well pleased."

I was getting a little exasperated. "Well, what is your solution to the problem?"

"I think in the next election we should have a right to vote for the President's aides, as well as for the President. If the country is going to be handed over to Haldeman, Ehrlichman, Charles Colson and John Dean III, the American people should know about it in advance."

"That makes sense," I admitted.

"And I believe they should be sworn in at the same time as the President. If the President swears to uphold the Constitution, his people should swear to it, too. Then if they screw up, we can impeach them in a package deal."

VI. SKELETONS IN THE CLOSET

THE TRIALS OF THE FORD FAMILY

One of the controversies swirling around Washington is whether Vice President Gerald Ford is thinking seriously about moving into the White House. It was started when John Osborne of the *New Republic* interviewed Ford, and the Vice President speculated about whom he would appoint to his Cabinet if he became President. This was followed by columnist William Safire's article in which Ford tried to clarify what he said to Osborne, which, or course, increased the speculation.

In fairness to the Vice President, particularly in view of what's going on in Washington, no one in his position could help thinking that he might be called to take on the reins of government, and the whole Ford family must be under tremendous strain.

I can just imagine what happens when the Vice President comes home.

He opens the door and hears music: "Who the devil is playing 'Hail to the Chief'?"

"We were just having fun, Jerry," his wife, Betty, says.
"Well, it's not very funny," Ford replies. "Suppose I had
walked in with the President?"
"Then we would have said we were playing it for him. You
look bushed. Do you want a drink?"
"Yes, give me a White House—I mean a White Horse—on
the rocks. What are all those swatches on the floor?"
"I was just looking at drapery material. You know the
drapes in the Lincoln Room are so ugly."
"Why are you looking at drapery material for the Lincoln
Room, Betty?"
"You have to order this stuff six months in advance. You
can't just get them by calling up Macy's."
"Betty, I don't think you should be ordering drapes for the
White House, even if it takes six months to get them. If I've
told you once, I've told you a hundred times there is
absolutely no way I will be President of the United States."
"Then why do you keep standing in front of a mirror every
night in a morning coat with your hand on a Bible repeating,
'So help me God'?"
"I thought you were asleep when I did that."
"How can I be when you keep talking in your sleep all night
long?"
"What do I say?" the Vice President asks nervously.
"You mumble over and over, 'Ask not what your country
can do for you, but what you can do for your country.' "
"Do I do that?"
"That's not the worst of it," Betty says. "You keep
stretching out your arms with your fingers in a V for victory
signal."
"Gosh, I hope the Secret Service men haven't seen me.
Betty, every Vice President dreams about being President of
the United States. It's only natural. I'll bet you Nixon even
dreamed about it at one time."
"Well, if you can dream about being President, why can't I
dream about being First Lady?"
"You can dream about it, but you shouldn't be ordering
things for the Lincoln Room."
"All right. I'll just keep the swatches . I'm sure if anything
happens, they'll put through a rush job for me."

"Where are the children?"

"Mike is working on his memoirs. He received a hundred-thousand-dollar advance for a book titled *Downstairs at the White House.*"

"But Mike's never been in the White House!"

"They don't want the book until Christmas, dummy."

"Holy smokes! Who put that 'Impeach Nixon' sticker on the window?"

"The maid. She already sold her story about Camp David to the *Ladies' Home Journal.*"

SELECTING THE VP

There has been a certain amount of consternation among Congressmen, Senators and Republican Party leaders over the manner in which President Nixon selected Gerald Ford as his new Vice President. If you recall, Mr. Nixon asked members of Congress, governors and party leaders to submit three names of people they thought he should appoint. Everyone now thinks they've been had because the President apparently had made his choice before the names were submitted.

I am happy to report that this is not the case. The lists played an important part in the President's decision.

This is what happened. All the envelopes containing the names of Vice Presidential possibilities were gathered up and flown by helicopter to Camp David where the President, Pat, Julie and David Eisenhower and Tricia and Ed Cox were waiting to count them. Since this was such a personal decision, the President wanted no one but members of his immediate family to be in on it.

The envelopes were dumped on the living-room floor, and everyone dove in with letter openers. The President had a yellow legal pad on his lap.

"Here's one from Bella Abzug," Julie said. "She lists Ralph Nader, Father Berrigan and Betty Freidan."

The President wrote down, "One for Nader, one for Berrigan and one for Freidan."

Pat was amazed. "Are you really writing those people down?"

"My credibility is at stake," the President replied. "I want this to be a completely honest election."

Tricia said, "Here's John Connally's ballot. He has only one name on it."

"Who is it?" the President asked.

"Well, it isn't Rockefeller."

The President gave one vote to Connally.

Julie Eisenhower said, "Here's Rocky's suggestion."

"Don't tell me," the President said. He marked one down for Rockefeller.

"Did you ask John Dean to submit any names?" David Eisenhower asked.

"Give me that," the President said and ripped the slip into shreds.

The counting went on during the night. Sandwiches and coffee were served as the family continued their arduous task.

As the evening wore on, the leaders in the balloting were Reagan, Goldwater, Rockefeller and Bill Rogers.

But many other candidates were mentioned. George Allen, the coach of the Redskins, got six votes; Judge Sirica got seven; Jimmy Hoffa got two.

"Here's an envelope from Archibald Cox," Pat said.

"Whom did he vote for?" the President asked.

Pat opened it. "It's not a ballot. It's a subpoena for your tapes."

"What a dirty way to serve it," the President said angrily.

"Did you ask Howard Hughes to submit a suggestion?" Eddie Cox asked.

"I did not," the President replied.

"Well, there's nothing in the envelope but fifty thousand dollars in cash."

"Send it back," the President cried.

About four o'clock in the morning the President tallied the votes as the family anxiously awaited the results.

"Well," Mr. Nixon said, "it looks like it's Jerry Ford."

"Jerry Ford?" Julie said. "But he didn't get three votes."

"I know, but I decided on Jerry Ford a week ago."

"Then why have we been counting ballots all night?" Tricia asked.

"I didn't want the people whom I asked to submit names to think I was wasting their time."

THE ALL-PURPOSE FORD SPEECH

Vice President Jerry Ford has been zigging and zagging on the question of impeachment for some time. It's a very difficult position for him to be in, and since he has to give so many speeches, it's hard for him to remember what he said the day before.

Because I admire the Vice President very much, I have written a standard speech for him which should cover all the bases.

It goes like this:

My fellow Americans,

I would like to say before I begin that I am neither for impeachment nor against impeachment. I believe that a little impeachment never hurt anybody. But if impeachment gets out of hand and starts to affect the country, then we should take another look at it and decide whether there is another way of resolving the issue which can accommodate the positions of those who are for it, as opposed to those who are against it.

Now let me say at the outset that on the basis of all I have read so far the President is not guilty of any impeachable offenses. At the same time, if he is withholding evidence which could show that he should be impeached, then he should turn this evidence over to the House Judiciary Committee and settle his guilt or innocence once and for all.

I have talked to the President on this very subject and expressed my views quite clearly. He has expressed his views to me. It's quite possible that on the basis of our discussions we may disagree.

But the fact that we disagree does not mean that we do not see the question in the same way. The President may have his reasons for not turning over the tapes to the Judiciary Committee, and I may have my reasons for him to get the whole thing out in the open. Because the President is stonewalling Congress does not mean that I do not support his efforts to do the right thing no matter if I personally believe it's the wrong thing.

I feel the House Judiciary Committee has enough evidence now to judge whether the President is guilty of high crimes and misdemeanors, and they shouldn't ask for any more evidence unless they believe they need the evidence to find out if the President is guilty or not. If they need it, then the President should turn it over to them, though I think it would be a mistake if the President turned over the material and it was then decided it wasn't the proof they needed.

Furthermore, and I have said this many times, the fact that the President has decided to refuse to give more evidence to the Congress should not be interpreted to mean he is hiding anything. I do not know if he is hiding anything because I have not heard the tapes. And I do not want to hear the tapes because if I heard them I would have to make a judgment as to the President's innocence or guilt, which would be a mistake if at some future date I would be asked where I stand.

I can tell you though that every time I have met with the President he has been in excellent health both mentally and physically, and I am impressed at his ability to see everything so clearly, although at times it doesn't seem very clear to me.

In conclusion, I would like to say that I will continue to support the President, although I may disagree with him. And I know he supports me. That's why he keeps calling me in to talk to him about why I am not supporting him. If he didn't respect me, he wouldn't try to change my mind. Would he?

SKELETONS IN THE CLOSET

Vice President Spiro Agnew met alone with President Nixon in the White House, and while the lid was put on their conversation, it is now coming out in bits and pieces.

"Spiro, there is something I meant to ask you five years ago when I chose you for Vice President, but it slipped my mind at the time: Do you have any skeletons in your closet?"

"I have never been treated for mental illness, if that's what you mean."

"That isn't what I mean, Spiro. I mean do you have any *other* skeletons in your closet? A horror that the press might grab hold of and make something out of?"

"I can't think of anything. My life is an open book."

"What about this business in Baltimore County that everyone seems to be talking about? Why didn't you tell me about that?"

"You didn't ask me."

"Yes, Spiro, I'm aware of that. But couldn't you have volunteered that information anyway?"

"Probably, but I was so excited when you called to offer me the Vice Presidency that it slipped my mind. Besides, it happened so long ago that I thought it didn't matter one way or another."

"Excuse me, Spiro, I have to change the tape. . . . All right, let's assume I made a mistake in not checking out the skeletons in your closet. We have to ɪace up to the fact that the skeletons are now out in the open. What should I do about it?"

"Why don't you announce that you support me a thousand percent?"

"I'd like to, Spiro. That would be the easy thing to do, the popular thing. But a President has to do a lot of things that are unpopular and will lose him votes. Spiro, I can't support you a thousand percent."

"Could you support me five hundred percent?"

"I wish I could, but my lawyers say that I can't afford to because the skeletons in *my* closet are beginning to haunt me."

"I was going to ask you in 1968, Mr. President, if you had any skeletons in your closet. I wish I had."

"Why is that?"

"With all due respect, sir, if they hadn't brought out the skeletons in *your* closet, they would never have brought out the skeletons in *mine.* "

"Are you trying to say my skeletons are responsible for your skeletons coming out of the closet?"

"Well, I was Mr. Clean until all that San Clemente and Key Biscayne business broke in the newspapers."

"I'm sorry, Spiro, I have to change the tape again. . . . Let's see, where were we? Oh, yes. As I understand it, what you're saying is that I am responsible for your troubles."

"I wouldn't put it that strongly. But if it hadn't been for that stupid staff of yours, our skeletons would still be hidden

in our respective closets. I must say, Mr. President, you blew
it with the Watergate business, and I don't see why I should
be the fall guy."

"What do you advise me to do, Spiro?"

"Resign. Let me be President, and then they can't lay a
glove on me."

"That's out of the question, Spiro, and you know it. If I
resign, what will happen to me?"

"Nothing. The first thing I'll do as President is give you
executive clemency . . . executive clemency . . . executive clemency . . . executive clemency . . . executive
clemency. . . ."

SEND IN A NEW KICKER

Playing Coach Dick Nixon paced up and down the sidelines of
the football field. His team was on his own ten-yard line, and
he was being forced to punt. To make matters worse, his only
kicker, Ted Agnew, had been thrown out of the game for
unsportsmanlike conduct and had been put on probation for
three years and fined $10,000.

Sitting on the bench, all suited up, were Johnny Connally,
Rocky Rockefeller, Ronnie Reagan, Bill Rogers, Mel Laird,
Barry Goldwater and Big Elliot Richardson.

"Send me in, Coach," begged Connally. "I can save the
game."

"I can't kick," Rocky said, "but if you need me, I'll run
with the ball."

Ronnie Reagan said, "Don't forget, I was the original
Gipper of Notre Dame."

Nixon just walked up and down the sidelines some more.

He was in a terrible dilemma. If he sent in a strong player,
the Democratic team vowed to block the kick. If he sent in a
weak player, he might lose the game.

He looked over at Johnny Connally. Johnny was his first
choice, but he was a problem for any coach. He had played on
the Democratic team until this year, and now that he was on
the Republican team, the Democrats seemed to have it in for

him. Nixon's scouts had informed him that if he sent in Connally, the Demos would smear him.

The crowd, shocked by Agnew's sudden departure from the field, kept screaming for a substitute.

But this punt meant a lot, and Coach Nixon was not about to be rushed. He walked to the Republican cheering section and said over the loudspeaker, "I need your help. Would everybody please list your three choices for a substitute kicker, put them in a sealed envelope and send them down to the field?"

The Democrats were furious. "How long are you going to have a time-out?" one of the players yelled.

Nixon ignored him and walked down past his bench.

Everyone looked up hopefully. Ronnie Reagan said, "Coach, I know your game plan, and I'm a team player. Give me a break."

Rocky said, "You have to send in someone whom the fans can rally around. You can't think of today, but of the big game in 1976. You won't be sorry, Dick."

Barry Goldwater played it cool. "I don't give a damn if you send me or not, Coach, but you could do a lot worse."

The fans were passing down their sealed envelopes, and Mel Laird started counting names. Every time he came across a list in which he wasn't mentioned, he threw it away.

Coach Nixon went up to Big Elliot Richardson. "Elliot, if I send you in, will you forget about the tapes I made of the other games?"

"It's hard to say, Coach. It's not up to me any more; it's up to the football commissioner."

Nixon turned away in disgust.

Mel Laird came over with the count. "The fans have voted forty-nine thousand seven hundred and sixty-eight for me, four for Connally, three for Rocky and one for Agnew."

A delegation from the Democratic bench started to cross the field. "Look, Dick," one of them said as he came up to Nixon, "you can't hold up the game forever. We can block any kicker you send on the field."

Nixon barked, "The rules say I have a right to choose any substitute I want to kick for me."

"But only with our approval," another Democratic coach

said. "Now we have a compromise. Why don't you use one of
our kickers? It could bring the stadium together."

"You're out of your minds," Nixon said. "You want me to
use a Democratic player on my team?"

The Democratic coach shrugged his shoulders. "It's the
only way you'll ever get to punt."

Nixon angrily turned to the bench and said, "Go in, Jerry,
and win this one for the Spiro."

THE DEMOCRATS ARE SUFFERING

The Democrats in this country were in a turmoil. Should they
support the President of the United States, the Vice President
or the Department of Justice?

McNulty, an ardent Democrat, told me, "We've never had
a problem like this. In the past, if you were against the
President, automatically you were against the Vice President.
And if you were the party out of power, you never trusted the
Department of Justice, either. But now that they're at each
other's throats, I don't know who to support."

"Do you have to support anybody?"

"Of course I do. What kind of American would I be if I
didn't take sides?"

"Well, whose side are you on?"

"I tend to lean toward Agnew emotionally, though my
sense of justice makes me want this matter settled in the
courts."

"Don't you have any sympathy for the President?"

"Of course. Nixon asked his Vice President to take a flying
leap out of the window, and Agnew refused to do it. It's very
hard to run the country if your own Vice President doesn't
follow orders."

"I'm not clear where you stand, McNulty."

"Neither am I. It's easy to put myself in the Vice
President's position. No one wants to jump out of the
window, even if he's ordered to do so by the President. At the
same time, if he doesn't jump, the President may have no
choice but to push him out."

"How do you know Nixon asked Agnew to take a flying leap out of the window?"

"Everyone knows *that*," McNulty said. "Don't forget there have been an awful lot of leaks coming out of the White House and the Justice Department. If we're to believe Agnew, there are people in the administration who are out to destroy him politically. I'm very sympathetic with him on this score. A man should not be tried in the press, particularly a Vice President."

"I'm glad to hear you say that, McNulty."

"At the same time, a man must not be allowed to escape punishment if he's committed a crime, which I'm not saying Agnew did. Had the Justice Department been more vigilant about Watergate, the American people would have known the truth about it at the very beginning."

"Who told you that?"

"Agnew said it in California. He said the reason he was being persecuted was that the Justice Department botched Watergate."

"Do you agree with that?"

"Not if I believe Attorney General Richardson's assurances that there is nothing personal in the grand jury hearings in Baltimore County, which could or could not produce an indictment of Agnew."

"I hope it doesn't," I said.

"I do, too, because it would place a great strain on President Nixon. It's not easy to keep the country's confidence when you have an indicted Vice President working for you, particularly one who won't resign."

"I hate to say this, but you seem to be fence-straddling," I said.

"It isn't my fault. The Republicans got us Democrats into this dilemma. We've never had to choose up sides between *their* President and Vice President before. I tell you it's driving me crazy with grief."

"You're just saying that, McNulty. You seem to be enjoying the whole mess."

McNulty got into his car, lit up a big cigar, smiled and said, "Who me?"

VICE PRESIDENT WANTED

Although President Nixon denied it at his press conference, the White House did have contingency plans in case Vice President Spiro Agnew resigned.

The search for another Vice President went on quietly, and no stone was left unturned to find the best man for the job.

The head of an executive employment agency in Washington told me he had received a call from someone in the White House.

The aide said, "We're looking for a Vice President of the United States. Do you have anyone on your rolls that we might interview?"

The agency boss said, "No, we don't have anyone listed who is looking for that kind of job. What does the Vice President do?"

"He doesn't do *anything*."

"Oh, that makes it rather difficult," the agency head said. "Does he have to know shorthand and typing?"

"No, he gets a secretary with the job; also his own staff, a limousine and the use of an Air Force plane. It also pays quite well."

"Let me go through my files. I have someone here. He was the vice-president of a large insurance company and ran the claims department. It says here he was indispensable to the company, and the president wouldn't make any important decisions without checking with the vice-president."

The White House aide said, "I'm afraid he would be overqualified for the job. Look, don't you have someone who is very presentable, likes to play golf, can make fund-raising speeches and won't bug anyone because he has nothing to do?"

"I'll check. Wait a minute. This may be the person you're looking for. He's forty-nine years old, very good-looking, is a fantastic speaker, a great athlete and is a nut about leisure time."

"That sounds pretty good. Where is he?"

"Well, he was indicted in some building scandal in St. Louis, but he'll be available right after his trial."

"No," said the White House aide, "on second thought I don't think he's the person we have in mind."

"I have a card on another executive here. He's now working for an oil company but wants to improve himself. He's a very attractive fellow, active in his church, involved with community affairs, has a lovely wife and is a lawyer by profession."

"He sounds good," the White House aide said.

"He also serves on the board of the National Association for the Advancement of Colored People."

"Oops! Who else have you got?"

"I don't know. Most of the people registered with us are very talented. I'm not sure they would be interested in a job that didn't have any responsibility. Say, wait a minute, there was a woman who came in the other day and—"

"Forget it," the White House aide said.

"I tell you what I'll do," the agency head said. "I'll start scouting around to see if I can find anyone with the qualifications you have in mind. I'm sure we can find someone to fill the job. Is there any chance for advancement?"

"You can tell your clients that if the person keeps his nose clean and doesn't bug anyone in the White House, he could move up to President of the United States in 1976."

"Say, I might even be interested in the job myself," the agency man said.

"What's your name?" the White House aide asked.

"Dean—John Dean, but I'm no relation to the one who—"

The White House aide slammed down the phone.

HENRY THE HUSBAND

The one question I keep getting asked when I'm on the road is "What kind of husband will Henry Kissinger make?" It's a hard one to answer, but on the basis of Henry's recent behavior, Mrs. Kissinger is going to discover that it isn't easy to be married to the supernegotiator of the world.

This is the kind of situation that could come up.

"Henry, I forgot to buy bread for the smoked salmon for our dinner party tonight. Would you go down to the supermarket and get a couple of loaves?"

Henry replies, "Of course, my dear."

He returns in a half hour. "What kind of bread did you want, rye or white?"

"It really doesn't matter, Henry. Either one will do."

"It's not going to be that easy. The supermarket has more white than it does rye, and therefore, they have put the white bread up in the front and the rye bread in the back. They're demanding guarantees that I buy two loaves of white for every loaf of rye. I've taken the position we should have the right to buy the rye bread without having to purchase the white bread."

"For heaven's sake, Henry, the guests are coming in forty-five minutes. Will you go back and get the bread?"

Henry comes back after fifteen minutes. "The supermarket has agreed to sell me the rye without having to buy the white, but they raised the problem of the size of the loaf. If we get the large loaf, we get three cents off, but that means we'd only need a loaf and a half. But if we get the small loaf, we'd need two, and the price would be prohibitive. What do you suggest we do?"

"Henry, I need bread for the dinner. Would you please go back and bring some home?"

Henry went back to the store and returned again.

"I think I've worked out a compromise, Nancy. If we get rolls instead of bread, we won't have the problem of choosing sizes. The supermarket has indicated it would consider selling us rolls at a special price, provided we buy a jar of peanut butter that they're pushing as part of a Fourth of July sale. I told them I would bring the offer back to you and lay it on the table."

"Henry, I don't care if it's peanut butter or jelly or cream cheese as long as you get the bread."

"They didn't raise the question of jelly or cream cheese, but I'll tell them you'd rather have that than peanut butter."

By this time several reporters who are standing outside the Kissinger home surround the Secretary of State. "Mr.

Kissinger," one of the reporters asks, "we understand you're trying to buy bread for your dinner tonight. Do you think you'll be able to do it?"

"There are still some last-minute details to be worked out," Henry says, "but I'm optimistic that there will be a deal."

But when Henry returns from the supermarket, he is glum and tells the reporters, "I would be less than candid if I told you that I brought back bread.

"The supermarket has raised some last-minute conditions on slicing that I'm not sure can be met. But after reporting to my wife, I am going back and make one more effort to find a compromise which both sides can live with."

By this time the guests are arriving and Nancy is crying. Everyone asks where Henry is, and Nancy doesn't have the nerve to tell them he's still out trying to buy bread for dinner.

Just as they sit down to dinner, Henry rushes in with three boxes under his arm. His face is flushed and he waves them at Nancy.

"Bread?" Nancy asks.

"Ry-Krisp," Henry replies. "But at least it's a start."

"By gum," says a reporter peeking through the window, "Henry's done it again."

THE VICE PRESIDENT'S BOOK

"Bob, there's a guy outside who says he's a former Vice President of the United States. He has an idea for a book he wants us to publish."

"I've got a lunch date."

"He has two Secret Service men with him. I think you'd better see him."

"Okay, send him in."

"How do you do? I'm the former Vice President of the United States, and I have this idea for a fantastic novel that surely would become a Book-of-the-Month."

"Could you give me some idea of what it's about?"

"Well, it takes place in 1983, and it's the story of a Vice President of the United States who is brainwashed by the

Chinese when he goes to Afghanistan. He is programmed to take over our country.''

"Gosh, we have three books like that right now. I don't think we'd be interested.''

"Well, what about a story on a Vice President who wants to fly, and everyone says he can't fly. But he's going to prove them wrong. Every night he jumps off the roof and falls. But finally one night he starts flapping his arms, and by God, he's soaring in the air.''

"It has possibilities, but I'm not certain it's our kind of book.''

"All right, then I've got another idea. The devil gets into this Vice President and makes him do and say terrible things. A priest is called in by the President and asked to exorcise the devil out of the VP. The priest in a very dramatic scene forces the devil out of the Vice President and into his own body and dies.''

"Yes, it's not a bad idea, but we stopped publishing devil books last year. I'm afraid our list for 1974 is complete.''

"Listen, I have lots of ideas. There's this Vice President of the United States and he tells how to be his own best friend. It's an uplifting book which would bring joy and inspiration to millions of people.''

"I'll discuss it at our next meeting, but please don't get your hopes up.''

"If you don't like that, how about *The Ex-Vice President's Diet Revolution?* It's a diet which permits people to eat all the fat they want, as long as they don't consume any carbohydrates.''

"We're up to our hips in diet books.''

"All right. Let me try this one out on you, *The Vice President's Joy of Sex.* It would be a frank book about how people could get more out of their sex lives, illustrated and sold for twelve ninety-five.''

"I really have a luncheon date, sir. Could you drop me a line about your ideas?''

"Wait, I'm not finished. I've had this idea for some time. There's this Vice President who is really a godfather and he has this family and there's another family trying to move in on his territory. So he orders a contract out on the other family, and you have this big gang war in Washington, D.C.''

"It's got possibilities, sir, but I doubt if it would sell."
"Well, what kind of book would you be interested in?"
"Just off the top of my head, we would be in the market for a nonfiction book about a Vice President who was a former governor of a state. During the course of an investigation of some contractors in the state, it's revealed that the Vice President took kickbacks from the contractors. Faced with the evidence, the Vice President is forced to resign the second highest office in the land. Would you be interested in writing that story?"
"I'm sorry, I couldn't write that kind of book. I wouldn't know where to begin."

HOW KISSINGER GOT MARRIED

The marriage of Secretary of State Henry Kissinger to the former Nancy Maginnes came as a surprise to everyone. Not even the Pentagon was let in on the secret, and members of the Senate Foreign Relations Committee are still mumbling that it was typical of Kissinger to do something like that on Saturday, when most Congressmen were out of town.

Although the State Department has remained mum on what led up to the marriage, I have been able to put pieces of the story together.

Kissinger came back from the Soviet Union on Thursday and immediately plunged into talks with Moshe Dayan in Washington. These talks were continued until lunch on Saturday.

At about noon Kissinger finished his conversation with Dayan, bade good-bye to him and then turned to his aide and asked, "What do I have on my schedule now?"

The aide said, "I don't see anything on your schedule, Mr. Secretary. You're free the entire afternoon."

Mr. Kissinger was incredulous. "What do you mean, I have nothing on my schedule? I always have *something* on my schedule. I think I'll go see the President."

"He's in Key Biscayne meeting with his lawyers," the aide said. "He can't see you until Sunday."

"All right then," Kissinger said, "I'll take a trip

somewhere. I think I'll go to India. I haven't been there in some time."

The aide replied nervously, "If you go to India this afternoon, you'll have to go to Pakistan as well, and you won't be able to get back in time for a reception at the Iranian Embassy on Monday."

"Well, is there any head of state visiting this country whom I can see?"

"King Hussein is in Palm Beach, but if you see him right after you saw Moshe Dayan, Sadat of Egypt might get angry."

Kissinger started pacing up and down the office.

"What about Africa? Couldn't I go to Africa this afternoon?"

"North or South Africa?"

"What difference does it make?" Kissinger asked. "Maybe I could work out a detente between the two of them."

"I wouldn't advise it, sir. If you go to Africa now, it will just stir up the Soviets and the Chinese."

"Chinese? There's an idea. Why don't I go see Chou En-lai? Get me Peking on the phone. . . . Hello, Chou. . . . This is Henry. I thought I'd come over for the afternoon, and we could have a bowl of rice together. . . . Oh, you've got tickets for the opera? . . . No, no that's all right. We'll do it some other day. . . . Yeah, sure, I'll give you some notice the next time."

Kissinger hung up the phone in despair. "Are there any movie premieres I could go to?" he asked his aide.

"You missed *The Great Gatsby* by three days," the aide said.

Just then Nancy Maginnes walked into the office.

"Hi, Henry, I was just driving by, and I stopped in to say hello. I won't keep you."

"No, no, sit down. I'm glad to see you. I don't have anything to do this afternoon."

"You must be kidding," Miss Maginnes said.

"I wish I was. My staff goofed up and left me without a trip, a negotiation or an appointment. I'm sick."

Miss Maginnes nodded sympathetically. "This is just a suggestion, Henry, but since you're free for the rest of the day, why don't we get married?"

Henry was shocked. "Married? It never occurred to me. I could probably get married this afternoon, couldn't I?"

"I'll check it out with protocol," the aide said, "but I'm sure they'd have no objection."

"Why not?" Kissinger asked Miss Maginnes. "It will be a fun way to kill the day before I go off to Damascus."

VII. RED FLAGS OVER WASHINGTON

BREZHNEV AND THE WATERGATE

Communist Party Chief Leonid Brezhnev met with Henry Kissinger recently at the Soviet leader's home outside Moscow. The conversation naturally got around to the Watergate, and this, in essence, is what was said.

"Gospodin Kissinger, I do not understand all this business about Watergate that is taking place in your country."

"Well, Mr. Brezhnev, it's rather difficult to explain. It appears that members of the President's political party bugged the headquarters of the opposition party."

"What's wrong with that, Gospodin Kissinger? We do it all the time."

"But you have no opposition party."

"That's true. So we bug our *own* party. You never can tell when our members are up to no good."

"In any case, Mr. Brezhnev, seven men were caught and tried for the crime. One of them confessed that higher members of the President's political party were involved."

"What is wrong with higher members of the President's

party finding out what the revisionist counterrevolutionaries are up to?"

"That's the way our people felt about it, too. But unfortunately some newspapermen got wind of the story and started to write about it."

"Why didn't the President put the newspapermen in insane asylums?"

"We cannot do that in the United States, Mr. Brezhnev."

"That's too bad. You cannot have order and discipline in a country if you are unable to put writers in mental institutions."

"That's true. The real problem, though, was that after the Watergate trial, it was revealed that members of the White House staff tried to obstruct justice and keep any higher-ups from being implicated."

"Naturally, Gospodin Kissinger. What other choice would they have?"

"In our country the people want to get to the bottom of things. They want to know who is responsible for a crime."

"Even if the President is involved?"

"Yes, sir, even if the President is involved."

"Why didn't President Nixon shoot everyone who had anything to do with Watergate, so that nobody would talk?"

"Some of the people involved were his best friends."

"In the Soviet Union, a leader has *no* friends. He must do what's right for the people even if it means losing a few bureaucrats."

"We're aware you do have a different system, Mr. Brezhnev, but we must deal with the Constitution. The President has to take responsibility for what his subordinates do, no matter how serious the crime."

"What kind of system of justice is that? The President should torture his subordinates until they confess he had nothing to do with it."

"We've thought of that, but it just wouldn't work in the United States because Congress would get wind of it and raise a storm."

"Why doesn't the President get the Army to arrest Congress?"

"We can't do it, Mr. Brezhnev. The people would never stand for it."

"In our country *we're* the people. And we arrest anybody we want to."

"I know, Mr. Brezhnev, I know. Now to get back to your meeting with President Nixon. . . ."

"I'm not sure I want to meet with a world leader who doesn't know how to bug his enemies without getting caught."

SEX VS. THE WATERGATE

I don't wish to put down our own Watergate affair, but when it comes to a good government scandal, the British have us beat by a mile. A recent British scandal had to do with sex.

It is the type of intrigue that even a charwoman can understand, having for its major characters Cabinet ministers, lords, dukes and call girls.

While our Watergate investigation has to do with who bugged whom, the British inquiry zeroed in on who slept with whom and for how much. And while the Senate drones on endlessly about what one lawyer told another lawyer in the Watergate break-in, the British scandal delved into the motives of why a man of title, wealth and position would pay for pleasure in the arms of a fallen woman.

What makes the British story different from Watergate is that all the major players kept a stiff upper lip. There was no begging for immunity, no taking the Fifth, no threats to implicate others.

When Lord Lambton, Prime Minister Heath's defense undersecretary, was confronted with compromising photographs of himself and a call girl named Norma Levy, he did not say he was doing it on orders from higher authority. Nor did he explain he took his action to protect national security. He did not hide behind the Union Jack.

He explained it simply on the BBC when asked by the commentator (and this is an exact quote, which shows you why British TV is so much better than ours), "Why should a man of your social position and charm and personality have to go to a whore?"

"Because," Lord Lambton replied, "I think that people

sometimes like variety. I think it is as simple as that and I
think this impulse is understood by everybody."

The main fear in the so-called Lambton affair was that state
secrets had been divulged during the liaisons. But Lord
Lambton squashed that on his BBC broadcast. "Businessmen
do not go with call girls to talk of private matters. If a call girl
suddenly said to me, 'Please, darling, tell me about the new
laser ray,' or, 'What do you think of the new Rolls-Royce
developments?' I would have known that something was up."

What also makes the Lambton scandal more interesting
than the Watergate is that there was more than one lord
involved. As a matter of fact, after Lambton, Lord Jellicoe,
the lord privy seal in Heath's Cabinet, admitted to having
affairs with call girls as well and tendered his resignation.
There was also a duke mentioned, and nobody knows how
many knights will eventually be involved.

I must say, the British newspapers took it very well. They
kept the public fully informed on every last detail of the
sordid affair, interviewing the call girls in question, the friends
of the lords, the wives and anyone else who could shed light
on what became the best story since the Profumo affair. As
far as British journalism was concerned, there would be no
cover-up.

Some Americans in London believe that the British broke
the story because they were jealous of Watergate.

"It was pure spite," an American State Department officer
told me. "Britain knew it couldn't be a major power without a
first-rate scandal, and the only way it could top us was to find
one with lots of sex in it. We consider the breaking of the
Lambton affair at this time as a very unfriendly act."

The only bright side of the story, from the United States'
point of view, is that although Lord Lambton wiped
Watergate off the front pages of Europe's newspapers, it's
hard to sustain a call girl scandal for very long.

Watergate, on the other hand, will probably go on for years.
Americans can take comfort that while Haldeman, Ehrlich-
man and Mitchell will remain household words for a decade,
Lord Lambton, Lord Jellicoe, Duke What's-his-name and
Norma Levy will soon be nothing more than a footnote in
Britain's long and illustrious sexual scandal history.

RED FLAGS OVER WASHINGTON

I was walking down Pennsylvania Avenue when I ran into an old man. His hair was white, and his beard was gray, and he was muttering to himself.

"Oh, my God. Oh, my God."

"What's the trouble, sir?" I asked.

"I never thought I'd see the day when the hammer and sickle would be flying from the Executive Office Building next to the White House."

"Don't get upset," I said. "It's just to honor Leonid Brezhnev's visit to the United States. He's the general secretary of the Communist Party in the Soviet Union, and he's visiting the President. Don't you read the newspapers?"

"I've been asleep for twenty years," the old man said. "Oh, my God, Richard Nixon warned us this would happen."

"You don't understand, old man. Nixon *is* the President, and he's the one who is entertaining Leonid Brezhnev."

"It couldn't be the same Nixon," the old man said adamantly. "The Nixon I knew sent Alger Hiss to jail for playing footsie with the Communists. In every political campaign he warned of the Red menace. He fought the Communists while everyone was being duped by them. Nixon would never entertain one in his home."

"Times have changed, sir."

"The name's Rip," the old man said.

"Well, since you've been asleep, a lot of things have happened. The President has even visited the People's Republic of China."

"Oh? How's Chiang Kai-shek?"

"Not *that* China, Rip. The other one—mainland Communist China."

"The President of the United States went to Communist China?"

"Yes, and then he went to Moscow. And he's sworn friendship to the Socialist People's Republic of the Soviet Union on Russian television."

"Oh, my God," Rip said. "Didn't Senator Joe McCarthy try to stop him?"

"McCarthy is dead."

"No wonder Nixon could get away with it," Rip said.

"Listen, Rip, I think I'd better clue you in on a few things. There is no such thing as a Red menace anymore. The President of the United States has made his peace with the two major Communist powers in the world. Communism is no longer a threat to the security of the Free World except in Indochina."

"Indochina?"

"Yes, we've been fighting a war in Indochina for ten years to keep the North Vietnamese Communists from spreading their insidious ideology over the globe. The President is committed to keeping them from achieving their goals."

Rip seemed confused. "That's the only threat of Communism there is in the world?"

"Exactly. All other forms of Communism, as far as President Nixon is concerned, are inoperative."

"Can my ears deceive me?" Rip said. "Is that the 'Internationale' I hear being played by the U.S. Marine Band on the White House lawn?"

"Yup," I replied. "They're playing *our* song."

"Oh, my God," Rip said. "Why did I ever wake up?"

"Don't worry, Rip, the détente with the Communist countries has been the greatest thing to happen in the last twenty years. It could mean a generation of peace for all mankind, except for those rotten Commies in Cambodia. If it hadn't been for Watergate, President Nixon might have gone down as one of the greatest Presidents in the history of our country."

"What's Watergate?"

"Rip, I think you'd better sit down. It's a very long story. . . ."

WHAT BREZHNEV LEARNED

Leonid Brezhnev stopped off to see French President Georges Pompidou on his way back to Moscow, and of course, they talked about their mutual friend, Richard Nixon.

"*Mon cher ami,*" said President Pompidou, "how was your visit to the United States?"

"Is fantastic!" said Secretary Brezhnev. "I was at the White House, Camp David and San Clemente."

"*Alors,*" said Pompidou, "when I met with Nixon, all I got to see was Iceland."

"Gospodin Pompidou, you should see the dacha Nixon has in San Clemente. It must be worth two, three million dollars."

"I didn't know he was doing that well as President."

"He doesn't do that well, but he has friends. He explained to me how he bought the place. It seems he has this friend Abplanalp who lent him the money to buy San Clemente. Then Abplanalp bought back everything but five acres so Nixon didn't owe Abplanalp anything. Nixon got the house for nothing, and Abplanalp got the land around San Clemente, and everyone was happy."

"It's hard for me to follow that," Pompidou said.

"Frankly, I didn't understand it either. But Nixon was laughing the whole time he explained it to me, so it must have been a good deal."

"How can he keep up three houses on his salary?" Pompidou asked.

"Is simple," Brezhnev replied. "Security."

"*Quelle* security?" Pompidou asked.

"Every time something has to be done to San Clemente dacha Secret Service says is for security. Nixon needs golf carts, is for security; new tiles for roof, is for security; heated swimming pool, is for security; beach cabana, is for security; electrical work on house, is for security. I tell you, Gospodin, when I get back to Soviet Union I am going to have a long talk with my security people and get my dacha by the Black Sea in shape."

"*Bonne idée!*" Pompidou said. "I think I'll meet with my security people and have them fix up my home at St.-Tropez. I could use a new guest house and a sauna."

"I am going to tell my security people to build me a movie theater and a golf course," Brezhnev said.

"Do you play golf?" Pompidou asked.

"No, but you never know when I'll be booted out by the

party, and a golf course should add to the value of my property."

"What else did Nixon tell you?" Pompidou wanted to know.

"He said the best investment he ever made was buying the dacha at Key Biscayne. He got the government to make five hundred seventy-nine thousand nine hundred and seven dollars' worth of improvements on this dacha, so if he ever wants to sell it, it will be worth three times what he paid for it."

Pompidou nodded. "I have always said about Nixon that he may not know how to protect the dollar abroad, but he really knows how to buy Florida real estate."

"You can say that again," said Brezhnev. "When I get back to Soviet Union, I'm going to speak to my good friend Bebe Rebozovitch and see if he can find me another dacha in Vladivostock with lots of security."

"Now tell me, Comrade Brezhnev, what did you find out on your visit to the United States that would be interesting for me to know?"

"Gospodin Pompidou, I will tell you something, but you must swear that you will never reveal where you heard it."

"*Sacre coeur,*" said Pompidou, "I swear it."

"Nixon has fantastic lawn-sprinkler system at San Clemente."

"*Alors!*" said Pompidou. "For security?"

Brezhnev shrugged. "What else?"

A GAP IN THE CANAL

The Middle East settlement hit a snag when it was discovered that 18½ miles of the Suez Canal were missing. Israelis who had custody of the canal could not explain what happened to the 18½ miles, but they did ask that the public withhold judgment until all the facts were in.

The UN special prosecutor's office is investigating the incident, the most serious to be revealed since the break-in of the waterway in 1967.

Experts who have been studying the canal insist the disappearance of the 18½ miles could not be an accident.

"Someone," an expert testified, "deliberately removed the portion of the canal to hide crucial evidence."

Reminded by the UN special prosecutor that the Israelis promised to turn over the entire canal for inspection, Avram Ben Igon, Moshe Dayan's personal lawyer, told the United Nations he had no idea what had happened to the 18½ miles. "It had been in a safe and guarded by our Secret Service for six years. Only four or five people had access to it."

Asked who they were the lawyer replied, "Moshe Dayan, General Bar Kochba, the Suez Canal custodian and Rose Mary Eban, Dayan's personal secretary."

Miss Eban testified she may have accidentally erased 5 miles of the canal with her foot when she was making a telephone call, but she couldn't explain what happened to the rest of it. She said she had worked on the canal at Mr. Dayan's request the weekend before negotiations between Egypt and Israel began.

She testified, "The canal was in very bad shape, and I had a very difficult time with it. After I made the telephone call and went back to measuring the canal, I realized it was short, and I immediately went to report it to Mr. Dayan. He didn't seem too worried and he told me, 'Don't worry, Rose Mary, the canal isn't important to peace negotiations.'"

UN observers, however, have maintained that the 18½ miles were indeed essential, and the disappearance of them might have an effect on the Arab oil embargo.

General Bar Kochba testified that only he and Dayan and Rose Mary had a combination to the safe where the canal was kept. "I believe some sinister force may have gotten into the safe and stolen the eighteen and a half miles. I remember giving Rose Mary the canal that weekend, but to the best of my recollection it was all there."

The missing portion of the canal is from Qantara to Ismailia, and Egyptian engineers maintain they will be unable to reopen the waterway until it is found.

The UN special prosecutor's office tried to question Mr. Dayan on his role in the affair, but he claimed executive privilege. His press spokesman, Ronald Allon, says that

Dayan knows nothing about the missing 18½ miles. "He had nothing to do with it, and he has ordered a full investigation to find out what happened. It's obvious that radical groups are trying to impeach Dayan over this minor incident. Mr. Dayan is sure that no one on his staff would have erased any portion of the canal to protect him from prosecution."

The gap in the Suez Canal caused great consternation in Cairo, Jerusalem and Washington, D.C. If it doesn't turn up in the next few days, Henry Kissinger may have to fly back to Kilometer 101 and start all over again.

UN observers refused to place guilt on any of the parties involved, but yesterday Moshe Dayan's aides told Rose Mary Eban, "I think you had better get a lawyer."

VIII. SLOWLY IN THE WIND

A TELEGRAM TO THE WHITE HOUSE

It has been revealed that the Committee for the Re-Election of the President sent thousands of telegrams to the White House supporting President Nixon's mining of Haiphong Harbor. The White House was then able to claim that the American people were in favor of the action by more than five to one.

"Hello, Operator. I wish to send a telegram to the President of the United States at the White House."

"Yes, sir. Is this to be charged to the Committee for the Re-Election of the President?"

"No, dammit, I want it charged to my own telephone number."

"Just a minute, I'm not sure we can do that. If you charge it to the Committee for the Re-Election of the President, we can give you a special group rate."

"I'm not interested in a group rate. I want to pay for this telegram in full."

"Well, here's the problem, sir. If you charge it through the committee, we can assure delivery. But if you send it on your own, it might take several days to get there."

"How's that?"

"The committee picks up the telegrams it sends and delivers them in its own truck. Of course, in order to qualify for this service, you would have to send a telegram *favorable* to the President."

"This telegram does not happen to be favorable to the President."

"Oh, dear, that could be sticky for us. The White House refuses to sign a receipt for telegrams that are unfavorable to the President."

"Well, I don't care if they sign for it or not. I just want it delivered. Now here's the text."

"Just a minute, sir. May I read you several form telegrams? You can send any one of them for seventy-five cents."

"No, I don't want to send a form telegram. Can't I just say what I want to?"

"The Committee for the Re-Election of the President won't like that."

"I don't give a hoot about the Committee for the Re-Election of the President."

"Well, we do. They're out best customers. They send a thousand telegrams to the White House every day. And they get very annoyed if someone sends one on his own."

"Look, just write down what I have to say."

"The President depends on their telegrams. It lifts his spirit to know the American people are behind him."

"But if all the telegrams are sent by the Committee for the Re-Election of the President, how does he know the American people are behind him?"

"The President doesn't know the telegrams come from the Committee for the Re-Election of the President, silly."

"But it's been in all the newspapers."

"The President doesn't read the papers. He just reads the telegrams."

"Don't you ever get telegrams from people who don't support the President?"

"Oh, once in a while someone calls in and takes issue with a particular Presidential decision."

"What do you do about it?"

"We take his number and report it to the Justice Department."

"What do they do with it?"

"They tap his telephone."

"Maybe I'd better not send this telegram after all."

"That's up to you, sir. After all, it's a free country."

CHARLES COLSON'S GRANDMOTHER

Before the Presidential election in 1972, Charles Colson, who had the reputation as the most ruthless man in the White House, said he would run over his grandmother, if necessary, to get Richard Nixon reelected President of the United States.

Not much has been heard of Mr. Colson's grandmother since November, 1972, and I've been wondering about her.

This scene keeps going around in my mind.

Colson drives up to his grandmother's house in his 1973 Buick, parks in the driveway and goes to the door.

His grandmother, still on crutches from the '72 election, answers the knock.

"How are you, Granny?" Colson asks, kissing her on the cheek.

"I'm coming along fine. The ribs are mending, and the doctor says my hip should be healed in a matter of months. I must say, Charles, when you ran over me with your car, you really ran over me."

"Now don't start complaining again, Granny. You know as well as I do that the President's reelection depended on my running over you."

"Charles, I never asked you this before, but did President Nixon know you ran over me to get him reelected?"

"No, he didn't, Granny. I never told him, and he never asked me."

"Why not?"

"I thought it best that he not know. Running over a person, even if it's your own grandmother, is considered a crime, and had the President known, he would have had to lower the boom on *somebody*."

"Did John Dean know you ran over me?"

"It was *his* idea. Any crime committed in the White House in the last five years originated with John Dean."

"When did the President first find out I had been run over?"

"As far as I can recollect at this point in time, it was either on December 21 or March 22 of 1972 or 1973. He was very upset about it and made a statement that the running over of people's grandmothers had no place in the American political system."

"Did he ask you at any time if you had run me over?"

"Not exactly. He just said, 'Bob tells me you're doing a good job, Charles.'"

"And from that you deduced he was upset?"

"It was a feeling I had. Haldeman just winked at me, so I figured the President knew about it.

"Granny, I don't have much time. I have to go before another grand jury. But what I came to see you about is this. President Nixon is in a lot of trouble. As you know, although I am no longer in the White House, my loyalty toward him has never wavered. I am determined that he survive Watergate no matter *what* it costs."

"You're a fine boy, Charles. Loyalty has always been a Colson trait. What do you plan to do to save the President?"

"Granny, would you step out in the driveway for just a moment?"

"Oh, no, you don't, Charles. I'm not going to fall for that one again."

"I promise to be careful this time, Granny. I'll make sure you only wind up with a couple of bruises."

"Charles, no one loves the office of the Presidency more than I do, and no one prays more ardently that the President can get out of Watergate intact. But I did my share when I got Mr. Nixon reelected. I see no reason why I have to be run over again, just to keep him from being impeached."

"For God's sake, Granny, what are grandmothers for?"

RESTORING THE PRESIDENCY

One thing that everyone in this country seems to agree on is that we must restore faith in the executive branch of the government. Although President Nixon has appointed new people to the White House, most of them are old faces that just have been moved around from one post to another.

What the nation needs desperately is someone in the White House who has the complete and unequivocal backing of all the American people—someone who has never been touched by scandal of any kind, whose credibility is unquestioned and who is a symbol of everything Americans believe their leaders should be.

The only one on the American scene to do this is Secretariat, the Triple Crown winner of the Kentucky Derby, the Preakness and the Belmont Stakes.

If President Nixon would appoint Secretariat to an important position in the White House, he would be going a long way toward his promise of cleaning house and restoring the image of the Presidency. Mr. Nixon would be saying to the American people, "You want new faces in the White House. I'm giving you a winner."

Now, before you scoff at my suggestion, I would like to point out there is a precedent for such an appointment. The Roman Emperor Caligula appointed his own horse as a proconsul to Rome. It's true Caligula did this to show his contempt for the Senate, but I don't think any self-respecting person believes that Mr. Nixon would appoint Secretariat for the same reason.

As a special assistant to the President, Secretariat could accompany the President to Camp David and San Clemente. Mr. Nixon could confide in him without fear that his conversation would be leaked to the press. And when the President gets tired and weary from all the affairs of state, he could ride Secretariat around the White House lawn.

The stallion could also fulfill other functions in the White House. When Press Secretary Ron Ziegler or his assistant,

Gerald Warren, receive a particularly tough question, they could say, "We'll check that out with Secretariat and get back to you later." Or if Secretariat can't answer it, they can always reply, "That's a horse of a different color."

Secretariat could show up for political fund-raising dinners and at Congressional hearings. He could get involved in the energy crisis and go to Paris with Henry Kissinger.

But his most important function would be that when the President's enemies call for his resignation or impeachment, Secretariat could warn the country that you don't change horses in midstream.

As President Nixon has said many times he would go to any lengths to clear up Watergate, Secretariat could supply him with thirty-one lengths to start with.

I have given reasons why President Nixon would want Secretariat in his Cabinet. But why would Secretariat take the job at this time?

The answer is that Secretariat is retired from racing and therefore would have no conflict of interests. Also, America has been good to Secretariat, and he would like to pay it back with some public service. He feels he still has a lot to give to this country.

When I suggested my idea to friends in the White House press corps, they were quite skeptical that Secretariat could restore faith in the Presidency. One said, "We've had horses in the White House before."

"Aha!" I said. "But this one has a head."

KUDOS

This is the time of year when honorary degrees are presented to men and women who have made their indelible mark on this country.

Here are some of the degrees which had been offered, but for one reason or other could not be accepted.

Watergate University

To G. Gordon Liddy and E. Howard Hunt—a doctorate in electronic communications. Their research into the Democratic Party headquarters broke new ground in understanding the American political process. Working from grants given by the White House and the Committee for the Re-Election of the President, their reports on Daniel Ellsberg's psychiatrist and various newspapermen in Washington are textbook classics in the science of gathering information against insurmountable odds.

Cash State College

Maurice Stans—a doctorate in political finance. He brought a new era to Mexican-American banking relations. In less than three months he managed to raise $20,000,000, most of which could not be traced to its donors. This brilliant coup, which may never be duplicated, has assured him a place in fund-raising history. The name Stans has now become synonymous with the $100 bill.

Martha University

John Mitchell—a doctorate in grand juries. As Attorney General of the United States, he brought law and order to a chaotic land. While serving as Attorney General and, afterward, as manager of the President's campaign, he used all his expertise in fighting crime to assure Mr. Nixon's reelection. Some may question his methods, but no one can deny that as architect of the election game plan he brought glory and honor to the Republican Party.

Washington Institute of Creep

Jeb Magruder—a doctorate in perjury. His boyish face and winning smile hide the heart of a Nixon loyalist who would do anything, and has, to protect the great office of the Presidency.

Although all his contributions to the campaign may never be known, suffice it to say whatever credit he gets for changing the manner in which we elect our future leaders, it is richly deserved.

Heidelberg University

H. R. Haldeman and John Ehrlichman—doctorates in heel clicking. As the President's closest advisers these two fun-loving aides endeared themselves to Congress, Cabinet officers and members of the administration. Their willingness to listen to others and their determination to keep the President fully informed as to what was going on fostered an atmosphere of trust in the White House. Although their memories are failing since they left the government, they are still considered the brains behind many of the national security plans President Nixon approved of during the past three years. Whether the Justice Department will give them their due is yet to be seen.

University of Obfuscation

Ronald Ziegler—a doctorate in freedom of information. As press secretary to the President he raised the meaning of credibility to a new level in the White House. No question was too hard to answer, no denial too difficult to make. He won the hearts and minds of all the media by adding the words "misspoke," "operative" and "inoperative" to the English language.

Scapegoat Institute of Technology

John Dean III—a doctorate in immunity. He has been an inspiration to all those who wish to devote their lives to public service. As legal adviser to the White House he kept the President informed on the great issues surrounding the 1972 campaign. Put in charge of the White House investigation into questionable practices by members of the President's staff, he worked diligently with the FBI and Justice Department to discover any wrongdoing.

To this day, President Nixon maintains he would not be where he is if it hadn't been for John Dean III.

SLOWLY IN THE WIND

Probably the worst part of John Ehrlichman's testimony in front of the Senate Watergate committee was when he denigrated the FBI and its late great leader, J. Edgar Hoover.

I couldn't believe my ears when I heard Ehrlichman say that the reason the President set up the plumbers unit in the White House was that he couldn't trust the FBI to do a thorough investigation of the Ellsberg case.

The day after Ehrlichman finished testifying I went to visit J. Edgar Hoover's grave. It was quiet and peaceful, and no one was there. I sat down on a stone bench and I said:

"J. Edgar, I know you're not going to believe this but people in the White House are saying terrible things about you. . . . Who? . . . Well, John Ehrlichman, for one. . . . No, he's not the thin guy with the brush hair. . . . That's Haldeman. Ehrlichman is the plump fellow with the big jaw who nods his head all the time whether you're asking him a question or not. . . . That's right, the baldish guy with the silly grin on his face. . . . Well, J. Edgar, he said President Nixon should have dismissed you early in his term because you couldn't do your job.

"I swear it, J. Edgar. I'll bring the record if you want to read it. Can you imagine someone from the White House saying that about you after what Nixon said at your funeral, that you were one of the greatest Americans of all time?

"I know you're asking why they would do such a thing, and I'll tell you why.

"They're beating a dead horse, if you'll excuse the expression, to justify setting up their crummy plumbers operation with G. Gordon Liddy and Howard Hunt. . . . Yeah, that's the one . . . the one you wouldn't approve of because it involved breaking and entering, forgery, arson and God knows what else in the name of national security.

"The things Ehrlichman said about you would make your hair stand on end. He testified you 'papered the files' and dragged your feet, and that your loyalty to your friends had priority over your loyalty to the country.

"I want to tell you that millions of patriotic, God-fearing Americans were shocked beyond belief when they heard those lies pouring out of his lips. Those of us who were brought up on your books and *Reader's Digest* and the television show *The FBI* couldn't believe anyone would accuse you of being soft on Daniel Ellsberg.

"There isn't a gangster, Nazi or Commie in this country who could say you were soft on anybody. . . . I'd like to see Ehrlichman talk to John Dillinger about your dragging your feet. . . . I'll tell you my theory, J. Edgar. I think Ehrlichman is trying to save his own neck and that of the President by using you to justify the White House break-in of Daniel Ellsberg's psychiatrist. . . . Ehrlichman kept saying they had to do it for national security because you refused to do your job.

"I know that statement is going to make you roll over in your grave. But I figured someone had to tell you what's been going on, since they put you out here.

"But don't worry, sir. Ehrlichman won't get away with it. The American Legion, the Veterans of Foreign Wars, the Daughters of the American Revolution and just plain old hundred percent Americans like myself are going to see that your reputation as the greatest crime fighter of all time is protected. No arrogant White House flunky is going to drag your name in the mud.

"When your successor, L. Patrick Gray, was fighting for confirmation on the Hill, Ehrlichman said he was just going to let Gray hang there and twist slowly, slowly in the wind. Well, that's exactly what we plan to do with Ehrlichman. We're going to let him hang there and twist, slowly, slowly in the wind.

"I thought you'd like that, J. Edgar. . . . Well, I have to be going now, but I'll come back and see you again. . . . Have a nice day."

THE GREAT LIDDY PLAN

One of the proposals G. Gordon Liddy is supposed to have made to the Committee for the Re-Election of the President was to hire call hirls during the Democratic National Convention and moor them on a yacht off Miami Beach. Liddy's plan, according to Jeb Magruder, was to lure Democratic politicians on board and photograph them in compromising positions.

The plan was vetoed by John Mitchell as being too expensive, but it probably wouldn't have worked anyway.

I talked to several Democratic politicians who attended the convention in Miami Beach, and they were appalled to think that anyone would believe that they would fall for such an obvious ploy.

One Senator told me, "If we saw a yacht with a bevy of girl volunteers on board, we would have known right away it was one of theirs. Hell, we didn't even have enough money for bumper stickers."

An aide to one of the Presidential candidates said, "We heard the Republicans were planning something like that, so we gave instructions to our staff to stick only to each other."

"I've heard of some dirty political tricks in my time," a Southern politician told me, "but putting beautiful, young, fresh, enticing, irresistible women at the disposal of the opposition party beats all. It is frightening to think that anyone in this country would use sex to pervert the great American political system. I hope we have learned a lesson from all of this, and that is when you try to buy an election with the bodies of voluptuous, breathtaking, willing women, you are making a mockery of the Consititution of the United States."

"Then," I said, "even if they had done it, you wouldn't have gotten involved?"

"I'm not saying that. If I saw a nice-looking yacht with some attractive ladies on board and they waved to me, I might have stopped by for a drink just to be sociable. After all, it was a damn hot convention. But if one of those lovely things asked me to go below deck to see the cabins, I would have replied, 'I would love to, young lady, but unfortunately I have to go and vote for Scoop Jackson.' "

A White House correspondent said he didn't think the Liddy plan would have succeeded without being exposed.

"Two hours after the yacht was moored, the word would have gone out that there was a hospitality suite serving more than drinks on the beach, and you would have had people standing in line all the way up to Fort Lauderdale. Somebody would have gotten suspicious and broken the story."

Another reason why he thought the plan would have failed is that the Liddy forces were so bad at electronics that they probably would never have been able to compromise the Democratic politicians on the first go-round. This meant the politicos would have to come back a second time, which for many of them would have been very inconvenient.

One young McGovern supporter told me that he had heard that the Committee for the Re-Election of the President was planning to provide girls free to Democratic officials, and he sought out Lawrence O'Brien, the Democratic National Committee chairman, for guidance.

All O'Brien told him was, "When the going gets tough, the tough get going."

Although the Liddy idea was vetoed, I was curious as to what such an operation would have cost the committee, so I sought out a madam who deals in luxury yachts.

"How much would it cost to charter a yacht with, say, ten girls on it?"

"If you have to ask," she said, "you can't afford it."

BIG JOHN'S IN TOWN

The town of Gemstone was all in a tizzy. Big John Connally was riding in on his palomino horse, sitting straight in the saddle, his eyes shaded by a large white hat.

He tied up his horse and walked into the saloon.

"Whatcha doing in town, Big John?" the bartender inquired.

"Come in to help Sheriff Dick Milhous," Big John said. "Understand he's been having a little trouble in these here parts."

"Nothing serious," one of the men at the bar said. "His deputies have been accused of cattle rustling, horse stealing, bank robbery, swearing and lying. Kind of tough on the sheriff 'cause he did so well in the last election."

"Ah'll straighten the whole mess out. All we gotta do is clean house, and everyone will forget what the deputies did. Guess ah'll wander over and see Dick now. Ah sorta would like to look over the place anyway, just in case ah want to run for sheriff sometime myself."

Big John walked across the street to the sheriff's office and knocked on the door.

"Sheriff, it's me, Big John. Ah came to help you out of your troubles. . . . Sheriff, you in there?"

There was no reply. Everyone was watching to see what Big John would do. He looked at them. "Is he in there?"

"Yup," one of men said.

Big John went around to one of the windows and tapped on it. "Dick, it's okay to open up the door. Ah'm here to help you save Gemstone."

There was still no reply.

Big John turned to the crowd. "You sure he's really in there?"

"Yup, he comes out once in a while and tells us he didn't know nothing about his deputies' cattle rustling, horse stealing, bank robbery, swearing and lying. And then he goes back in and locks the door."

There was a commotion at the courthouse next to the saloon. "What's going on there?" Big John asked.

"That's the deputies. They keep being called into the court to testify against each other. Lot of stuff went on in this town in the last year nobody knew anything about," a cowboy said. "They would have stole the town square if it hadn't been nailed down."

"There's got to be some way ah can get in to see the sheriff," Big John said. He climbed up to the second-floor balcony and peered in. Then he shouted, "Now look here, Dick, ah rode all the way in from Houston to give you a helping hand. You jes' open up that door and let me in!"

Dead silence.

"He ain't coming out," a man said. "You're wasting your breath. He's mad at everyone, especially the Gemstone *Post* for writing all about it."

"Sheriff!" Big John shouted again. "What in tarnation did you have me come up here for if you won't listen to what ah got to say?"

The crowd started laughing. "Big John, how you ever going to become sheriff of this place if the present sheriff won't even talk to you?"

Suddenly the window opened a crack, and Sheriff Milhous poked his nose out. He talked to Big John for about three minutes and then shut the window again.

Red-faced, Big John climbed down from the balcony.

"What'd he say?" someone in the crowd asked.

"We had a nice friendly chat, and ah think it did us both a lot of good."

Then Big John untied his horse and got back into the saddle and started riding out of town.

"Ain't you staying around, Big John?" a voice shouted.

Big John didn't reply. He just rode off into the sunset.

GOOD JOB, JOHN

The White House would have us believe that John Dean III, *by himself* and without aid, comfort or advice from anyone, conspired to activate the Watergate break-in and then cover it up so no one would ever know that people in President Nixon's administration were involved. The way they make it sound, Dean answered to nobody.

All right, let's raise that one up the flagpole.

PRESIDENT: John, Bob Haldeman just told me what a wonderful job you're doing.

DEAN: Thank you, Mr. President. But frankly I don't think it was Bob's job to tell you *anything*.

PRESIDENT: I'm sorry about that, John. Tell me, just out of curiosity, what have you been doing that Bob considers such a wonderful thing?

DEAN: I'm not at liberty to tell you, Mr. President. It's *very* confidential.

PRESIDENT: But I'm the President of the United States. Shouldn't I know?

DEAN: Mr. President, when it's time for you to know, I'll inform you. In the meantime, get off my back.

PRESIDENT: I didn't mean to offend you, John. I was just trying to get some information on a matter that will probably affect me sooner or later.

DEAN: This is a security problem, and as your counsel I cannot discuss it with you, Bob Haldeman, John Ehrlichman or anybody else. Now I'm very busy, and if you have nothing more to say, I'm going back to my office.

PRESIDENT: I didn't mean to take up your time, John. Could you give me a teensy-weensy hint as to what you're working on?

DEAN: Mr. President, You know very well I can't do that. If you don't feel I'm doing a good job, get yourself another lawyer.

PRESIDENT: I don't want another lawyer. I want you, John.

But you can't blame me for wanting to know what's going on around here.

DEAN: Why don't you ask Haldeman if he's so smart?

HALDEMAN: Mr. President, all I know is John is doing a good job. I never asked him *what* he was doing.

PRESIDENT: Well, how do you know he's doing a good job then?

HALDEMAN: Just by the way he keeps his desk. He's probably one of the neatest men in the White House. I always know a man's doing a good job when he doesn't have any papers on his desk.

DEAN: Oh, yeah? Well keep your nose out of my office, Haldeman. I might have something in there I don't want you to see.

PRESIDENT: Please, men, no fighting. We're one happy family in the White House. Right?

DEAN: I suppose so.

PRESIDENT: Let me ask you one more question. Are you absolutely sure, John, that there is nothing I should know concerning the people who work for me?

DEAN: Boy, you never give up do you, Mr. President?

HALDEMAN: If we thought you were going to get so upset, John, we never would have called you into the Oval Office.

DEAN: I'm sorry. I guess I've been working too hard, what with covering up and—

PRESIDENT: Covering up?

DEAN: You know what I mean. It gets cold at night in Alexandria, and my wife always keeps telling me to cover up. Well, I'll see you later. (He exits.)

PRESIDENT: Bob, I like that kid. He's a team player.

HALDEMAN: He's the salt of the earth, Mr. President. I wish we had a hundred like him.

PRESIDENT: Send him an electric blanket as a gift from me. I don't want him to catch cold.

WHAT TO SAY ABOUT WATERGATE

These are difficult times for people who are defending the Nixon administration. No matter where they go they are attacked by pseudo-liberals, McGovern lovers, heterosexual constitutionalists and paranoid John Dean believers.

As a public service, I am printing instant responses for loyal Nixonites when they are attacked at a party. Please cut it out and carry it in your pocket.

1. Everyone does it.
2. What about Chappaquiddick?
3. A President can't keep track of *everything* his staff does.
4. The press is blowing the whole thing up.
5. Whatever Nixon did was for national security.
6. The Democrats are sore because they lost the election.
7. Are you going to believe a rat like John Dean or the President of the United States?
8. Wait till *all* the facts come out.
9. What about Chappaquiddick?
10. If you impeach Nixon, you get Ford.
11. The only thing wrong with Watergate is they got caught.
12. What about Daniel Ellsberg stealing the Pentagon Papers?
13. It happens in Europe all the time.
14. People would be against Nixon no matter what he did.
15. I'd rather have a crook in the White House than a fool.
16. LBJ used to read FBI reports every night.
17. What's the big deal about finding out what your opposition is up to?
18. The President was too busy running the country to know what was going on.
19. What about Chappaquiddick?
20. People who live in glass houses shouldn't throw stones.
21. McGovern would have lost anyway.
22. Maybe the Committee for the Re-Election of the President went a little too far, but they were just a bunch of eager kids.
23. I'm not for breaking the law, but sometimes you have to do it to save the country.
24. Nixon made a mistake. He's only human.
25. Do you realize what Watergate is doing to the dollar abroad?
26. What about Harry Truman and the deepfreeze scandal?
27. Franklin D. Roosevelt did a lot worse things.

28. I'm sick and tired of hearing about Watergate, and so is everybody else.

29. This thing should be tried in the courts and not on television.

30. When Nixon gives his explanation of what happened, there are going to be a lot of people in this country with egg on their faces.

31. My country right or wrong.

32. What about Chappaquiddick?

33. I think the people who make all this fuss about Watergate should be shot.

34. If the Democrats had the money, they would have done the same thing.

35. I never trusted Haldeman and Ehrlichman to start with.

36. If you say one more word about Watergate, I'll punch you in the nose.

A. (If the person is bigger than you) If you say one more word about Watergate, I'm leaving this house.

B. (If it's your own house and the person is bigger than you) What about Chappaquiddick?

MY WATERGATE FANTASY

Everyone has his favorite fantasy after watching the Watergate hearings. I got mine when I watched Tony Ulasewicz testify how he left manila envelopes filled with $100 bills in phone booths and airport lockers to pay off defendants and lawyers involved in the trial.

My fantasy is that I have to call my wife, so I walk into the lobby of a lawyer's building and head for a public phone booth. I dial my number and get a busy signal. I hang up, wondering how long she'll be on the phone. Then I notice a plain brown envelope taped to the side of the phone. I tear it open and find inside a wad of $100 bills.

I immediately call my wife again. "Remember I told you this morning we couldn't buy any steak for a month? Well, that statement is inoperative. Go out and get six of the most beautiful sirloins you can find." I look in the envelope again. "And you can buy some lettuce, too."

"But we can't afford it," she protests. "I just bought a dozen eggs."

"Don't argue," I say. "We're going to eat steak for a week."

I hang up, shove the envelope in my inside coat pocket and nonchalantly leave the booth.

A burly man with a part in the middle of his black, greasy hair comes up to me. "What are you doing with that manila envelope?"

"What business is it of yours?"

"It's my envelope."

"It doesn't have your name on it."

"If you don't give it to me, I'll break your knees with a baseball bat."

Just then a man comes out of the elevator and goes to the phone booth. He searches it and comes out looking puzzled. Then he comes over to the burly man and says, "I thought you told me my legal fee would be in the phone booth."

"It was in the booth," the burly man says, "but this joker took it out, and he won't give it to me."

"There's a law against stealing someone's fee," the lawyer says.

"Show me where there is anything in this manila envelope to indicate this is a lawyer's fee," I reply.

"Well, for one thing," the lawyer says nervously, "I always get paid in hundred-dollar bills."

"In a phone booth?"

"Our accountant is on vacation." He blushes.

The burly man says, "I better call Mr. Novak." He goes into the booth.

"Who's Mr. Novak?" I ask the lawyer.

"That's the code name for Mr. Kalmbach, the President's lawyer."

The burly man speaks into the phone. "Mr. Novak, this is Mr. Rivers. . . . No, I didn't pay the lawyer because some guy picked up the lettuce in the phone booth before the lawyer got there. . . . The guy won't give it back. . . . Should we turn him over to the plumbers? . . . well, you better talk to him because I'm going to break his arm. . . . Hey, Mac, Mr. Novak wants to speak to you."

I take the phone.

"What's your name?" Novak asks.

"Gemstone Sedan Chair II," I reply.

"I understand you found twenty-five thousand dollars in cash in a phone booth."

"That's correct," I reply. "And as a lawyer you should know whatever someone finds in a phone booth belongs to him."

"It does not," he says. "It belongs to the phone company."

"Okay, I'll give the twenty-five thousand to the phone company."

"*No*. Don't do that," Mr. Novak says. "All right, let us for the moment assume the money is yours. Would you be willing to donate it to a defense fund for the poor families and starving lawyers who are trying to help the misguided individuals who broke into the Democratic headquarters early in the morning on June 17?"

"Nope."

"Give me Mr. Rivers again."

Rivers takes the phone. "I gotcha, Mr. Novak. . . . Let. the guy keep the twenty-five thousand and leave another twenty-five thousand in the phone booth for the lawyer. . . . I'm sorry, Mr. Novak, for the botch-up. . . . Yes, I agree with you. . . . There just aren't any honest people in the world anymore."

WHAT WE KNOW ABOUT WATERGATE

While all the facts about Watergate have not come out yet, it is time to sum up some of what the country knows about this fascinating affair.

The average cost of a White House aide's honeymoon is $4,800.

It cost American Airlines $100,000 to fly Herbert Kalmbach from New York to Washington.

John Mitchell, who told the country to "judge us by what we do, not what we say," can't remember what he did.

The *only* person in the Nixon administration in whom the country still believes is Julie Eisenhower.

No one approved of G. Gordon Liddy's plan to break into the Democratic Party headquarters. He did it on his own, against the protests of everyone in the White House and the Committee for the Re-Election of the President.

The best time to go to the bathroom while watching the Watergate Senate hearings was when Senator Joseph Montoya was questioning the witness.

No one talked to the President of the United States from June 17, 1972, until March 22, 1973, about his own political campaign.

It takes $20,000,000 to get an incumbent President *nominated* by his party for a second term.

The only person in the Watergate affair who doesn't have a good lawyer is the President of the United States.

If you commit a crime involving the administration, the first thing you should ask for is immunity.

John Ehrlichman's favorite hobby was recording the conversations of people who came to his office.

E. Howard Hunt has a thing about red wigs.

John Dean was running the White House alone for the past year.

The CIA does not launder money in Mexico.

L. Patrick Gray might now be head of the FBI if he only knew enough not to burn state's evidence.

The biggest problem the Nixon administration faced in the first four years was how to prevent an "enemy" from eating dinner at the White House.

If Charles Colson didn't like you, you could expect an audit by IRS.

The White House did not earn interest on the $350,000 kept in H. R. Haldeman's safe.

Had the President known what was going on in regard to the Watergate, according to John Mitchell, he would have taken action and would have lost the election.

Senator Howard Baker, as far as the American housewife is concerned, is the "cutest" member of the Ervin committee.

When people commit a burglary for a political party, their lawyers' fees should be paid in cash and their families should be taken care of, for "humanitarian" reasons.

The way to get back at someone who steals papers from the Pentagon is to raid his psychiatrist's office.

Men who have short hair and wear coats and ties are capable of lying.

If the President hadn't maintained three White Houses, he would probably have found out about the Watergate.

The two favorite phrases to come out of the Watergate hearings are "to the best of my recollection" and "at that point in time."

It now turns out that Martha Mitchell was not telling the truth when she said that whatever her husband knew about Watergate, the President knew as well.

MY SUMMER VACATION

The first thing everyone had to do when he returned to school in Washington was write a composition, "What I Did on My Summer Vacation."

Here are a few of the better ones.

Dickie Nixon wrote:

I went to San Clemente and Camp David and Key Biscayne. And we even made a side trip to Washington, D.C. At San Clemente we have a swimming pool and beautiful shrubs and gardens and new carpeting in all the rooms. I traded my collection of baseball cards with my best friends, Bebe Rebozo and Bobby Abplanalp. In exchange for the baseball cards they gave me a $600,000 loan. Then they gave me back most of the cards.

At night I listened to my tapes. I like the John Dean ones best. Everyone wants me to trade my tapes, but I'm not going to let anyone have them. I'm going to keep them forever and ever.

I didn't make many friends this summer. In fact, I lost some. But that's because everyone was saying mean things about me. I made a list of enemies, and this fall I'm going to get Sammy Ervin if it's the last thing I do.

I guess it was a rotten summer if you look back on it. But it's behind me, and now I have football to look forward to. When I

grow up, I'm going to be President because you can call up any
football coach and give him a play, and he has to use it whether
he wants to or not.

Teddy Agnew wrote:

I played golf this summer at Palm Springs with my best
friend Frankie Sinatra. I also played tennis. Then I had to go
back to Washington because some people said I had my hand
in the cookie jar in Baltimore. This is a big lie and got me very
mad.

I never took any cookies in Baltimore. Other people who
took cookies said I took them, but nobody asked me if I took
any. I received a letter from the principal saying that they were
looking into the fact that I had stolen the cookies. What I think
happened is that there are certain kids in school who don't
want me to be elected class president. So they leaked the story
about the cookie jar. I'm not going to take it lying down.

All in all I had a lousy vacation.

Little Martha Mitchell wrote:

I couldn't leave my house this summer because I was a
prisoner, so all I did was make telephone calls. I called my best
friend Helen Thomas and I told her what a goddamn fool John
was for protecting Dickie Nixon. John thinks if he doesn't rat
on Dickie, he won't go to reform school. But Dickie doesn't
care about anybody but himself. When classes start, I'm going
to tell Sammy Ervin everything I know about Dickie.

If I'm a good girl, John says I can go to camp next summer.
Big deal.

Henry Kissinger wrote:

I got a new job, and I met a lot of new girls, and I had a good
time. I bugged some friends, but no one got mad at me because
I explained I did it for their own good. I went to Hollywood
and met a lot of movie stars. I also got a nice tan. I was going to
go to China, but I went to Paris instead. I like to travel a lot.
My mother said if I got straight A's this year, she would give
me a subscription to *Playboy* magazine. I'm going to study
very hard.

HAIL TO THE CHIEF

Commander in Chief Nixon's hopes for a cease-fire on the domestic front failed when the press laid down another heavy artillery barrage in reply to a Nixon attack on a division of TV commentators.

Military observers now feel that the Commander in Chief is hopelessly surrounded. With Congress pressing hard from one side, the courts from another and the press dropping bombs every day, Nixon is being urged to surrender.

How did the Commander in Chief get himself into such a fix? General Southerwaite Sampson, a military historian, gave me his analysis of the situation.

"The commander, in November, 1972, had the strongest forces in the land. There was no opposition to speak of, and he believed that, with his loyal officers holding the White House and the Justice Department, no one could touch him. His first move was to make a preemptive strike against Congress. He impounded their money, and then he launched one veto after another at them until he had them on their knees.

"But just when victory was in his grasp, dissension broke out among Nixon's own officers. Some confessed that they were part of a scheme to destroy the honor of the country. Several who were court-martialed revealed that they participated in illegal acts with the knowledge and complicity of the Commander in Chief's staff.

"There were rumblings among the enlisted men that corruption had reached the highest levels of Nixon's army.

"The commander, under pressure, was forced to ask for the resignations of his most loyal aides.

"While trying to straighten out his own army, Nixon was unprepared for an attack by Congress. Airborne members of the First Senate Watergate Committee dropped behind his lines and started sniping at him from the rear. The press, which had been neutralized for four years, suddenly went into action and captured top-secret documents which implicated everyone in the high command in some kind of corruption.

"The attack by Congress and the press dispelled certain myths that had been built up in the world. One was that Congress wouldn't fight, and the other was that the press would flee when faced with the superior forces of the Justice Department.

"Having surrounded him, Nixon's enemies were demanding that he surrender tapes which could or could not implicate him in treachery. He refused and threatened to use the most powerful missile in his arsenal, executive immunity. But when he launched the missile, it fizzled and fell to the ground with a thud.

"In the meantime, several of his officers in the Fifth Justice Department Regiment mutinied and refused to obey Nixon's orders. He had no choice but to fire them. Then, in order to save what was left of his forces, he surrendered the tapes.

"But it was too late. The commander's legal army without discipline or leadership was unable to break him out of the trap he had gotten himself into.

"On Friday, Nixon in a last gasp mounted a counterattack against the press but was repulsed with heavy losses. It was the bloodiest battle so far."

"How is the Commander in Chief taking all this?" I asked Sampson.

"I've never seen him cooler," he replied. "Nixon thrives on adversity and expects to be out of his bunker at Camp David by Christmas."

THE CASE OF THE MISSING MANDATE

President Richard Nixon was elected with the largest mandate in American history. You can imagine his surprise recently when he discovered that it had disappeared. The President called his good friend Lieutenant Columbo of the Los Angeles police force to come to the White House.

"Hi there, Mr. President," Columbo said. "What's been going on?"

"Well, had you seen the newspapers, you would have read that my mandate has disappeared."

"What do you know!" Columbo whistled. "How valuable was it?"

"There was nothing like it in the country. It was fourteen-carat solid gold. Lieutenant, I'll do anything to get that mandate back, and I mean *anything.*"

"Whoa, Mr. President! Let's not lose our cool. Now, when was the last time you or members of your staff saw this mandate?"

"Well, as you know, I bought it on November 7, 1972, for more than 50 million dollars. I had it right here in the office through May or June of '73. Then suddenly I didn't see it anymore. I thought someone in the White House was having it cleaned, and I didn't think anything of it. But now it really does seem to be gone. I'm afraid it may have been stolen."

"Then you don't think you lost it?"

"What are you implying by that?" the President asked coldly.

"Now don't get sore, Mr. President. I have to ask these questions. It's my job."

"Well, you just find my mandate and get it back here right away," the President said.

A few days later Columbo opened the President's office door. "Oh, excuse me. I hope I'm not intruding."

"Don't you ever knock?" the President remarked.

"I knew I forgot something. My wife always says to me, 'Columbo, why don't you knock before you open a door?'"

"Did you find my mandate?"

Columbo walked over to the window. "It's the funniest thing. I put out an all-points bulletin to fifty states and no one has seen your mandate in months. Of course, Massachusetts never saw it at all. But the reports from the other forty-nine states were very discouraging. They said they all had seen it and then suddenly—poof!—it was gone. Let me ask you this. Could Spiro Agnew have taken your mandate when he left the Executive Office Building?"

"Hardly," the President said. "If you had seen the size of that mandate, you would have known that no one could get it out by himself."

"What about this fellow that you fired—Archibald Cox?"

"I've always suspected him of stealing my mandate. He

and Richardson and Ruckelshaus could have stolen it while I was at Key Biscayne."

"I doubt it, Mr. President. The way I figure it, whoever stole your mandate did it before October—sometime in the summer, like when the Watergate hearings were going on and everyone's attention was diverted. How about Mitchell, Stans, Haldeman and Ehrlichman? Could you see them robbing you of your mandate?"

"Impossible. They were my dearest and closest associates," the President said.

Columbo was walking around the Oval Office. He stooped down by a cut piece of wire. "What's this?"

"That's just a piece of wire. I used to tape everyone who came into my office."

"Where are the tapes now?" Columbo asked.

"In my bedroom, except for two that are missing."

"That's it!" Columbo said. "Whoever stole the two tapes probably stole your mandate."

"No, that can't be it," Nixon said. "The tapes don't exist."

"Are you putting me on?" Columbo asked.

"Sit down, Lieutenant. I know it's going to be hard for you to believe this, but. . . ."

BITE YOUR TONGUE

A lot of people have said a lot of things they are now sorry for. For example:

How would you feel if you had been the person who said to the Shah of Iran, "No, thank you, Your Highness, we don't need any oil. Go peddle your surplus somewhere else."

Or the one who advised President Nixon, "Why don't you release your tax returns? What have you got to hide?"

Or the Secret Service man who said to the contractor at San Clemente, "Why don't you put in a new furnace while you're at it?"

Or the Sony tape machine salesman who told his

customers, "Confidentially, the White House uses one just like it."

Or the real estate man who said to Spiro, "Well, as long as you're going to be Vice President for four more years, you might as well invest in a two-hundred-thousand-dollar home in Kenwood, Maryland."

Or the broker, any broker, who told his clients, "You couldn't do any better with your money than investing it in the stock market in October."

Or the lobbyist who said to a friend, "Don't waste your time with Jerry Ford. He isn't going anywhere."

Or perhaps the White House lawyer who said to President Nixon, "If you fire Archibald Cox on Saturday, no one in the country will know you did it."

Or the other White House lawyer who assured Mr. Nixon, "Don't worry about the missing tapes. Once you explain it, everyone will believe you."

Or the White House press agent who burst into the Oval Office and said, "I've got it! I've got it! We'll launch a counteroffensive and call it Operation Candor!"

Or the Israeli intelligence officer who assured Golda Meir's Cabinet, "You have my word, the Arabs are not prepared to fight."

Or the Egyptian intelligence officer who assured Sadat's Cabinet, "You have my word, the Israelis will never be able to cross the Suez Canal."

Or the American intelligence officer who told the National Security Council, "The Arab oil embargo talk is all bluff. What are they going to do, drink the stuff?"

Or the British minister who told Prime Minister Heath, "Sir, the country has just come to a halt."

Or the General Motors vice-president who told his bosses last spring, "My advice is to double the number of big cars we plan to make for 1974."

And how about the friend who said to John D. Love, "If I were you, I would resign as governor of Colorado and take the job as energy czar. What have you got to lose?"

Not to mention the political adviser to John Connally who said, "If the President wants you as Vice President, Congress can't do a damn thing about it."

Lest we forget the associate of Bebe Rebozo who told him, "If you give the one hundred thousand dollars back to Howard Hughes in cash, no one will find out about it."

Or the person who said to Rose Mary Woods, "This will give you a chuckle. They're going to have some young, miniskirted girl lawyer question you about the tape. Ha ha ha ha."

Or the Washington lawyer who told the Committee for the Re-Election of the President, "Don't worry about Sirica. He's the dumbest judge on the bench, and he'll believe anything we tell him."

And, finally, every poor soul in this country who said, "I have nothing against Billie Jean King, but I'll have to bet my money on Bobby Riggs."

IX. THOSE WERE THE DAYS

THE OIL VILLAIN

Who was responsible for the energy crisis? Many people
blamed the oil companies. Others blamed the government.
The automobile companies blamed the environmentalists, and
the Democrats blamed Watergate.

But Professor Heinrich Applebaum of the Yale Divinity
School told me who the real villain of the fuel crisis was. It's
the Harvard Business School.

The professor said, "Almost every sheikh now in charge of
oil policy for his country was trained at Harvard. Everything
they learned there they have put into practice to the detriment
of the free world. The Harvard Business School taught the
sons of Arab potentates how to sell oil, raise prices and
demand outrageous profits for the black gold they have in the
ground. Had these same sons been sent to the University of
Alabama, Oklahoma or Texas, they would now be involved in
developing football teams instead of putting the screws to
everyone."

"Then you think it was a mistake to accept Arab princes at Harvard?"

"It was an absolute disaster. We should have sent them to colleges where the kids swallowed goldfish, got involved in panty raids and drank Boone's Farm apple wine until six o'clock in the morning. We should have made them join fraternities and take sorority girls to beer busts.

"All the Harvard Business School did for the sheikhs was teach them the laws of supply and demand and the value of fuel in an industrial society."

"I guess at the time it seemed like a good idea," I said.

"It was never a good idea," Applebaum said. "Before Harvard started accepting Arab oil princes, their fathers were willing to own twenty-five percent of the wells and were happy to accept air-conditioned Cadillacs as presents. Then the Harvard Business School started turning out oil ministers that demanded full control of the wells, triple royalties and F-5 fighter planes. I assure you they didn't learn that in the deserts of Arabia.

"Every economics professor and business law teacher in Cambridge must bear full responsibility for the mess we're in," Applebaum said.

"But maybe the professors just thought they were teaching theory as far as the free enterprise system goes, and that it would never be put into practice."

"You don't teach theory to people who control seventy percent of all the oil reserves in the world. We should have sent them all to the Juilliard School of Music, where they could have learned to play an instrument."

"Who gave the sheikhs the idea to send their sons to the Harvard School of Business in the first place?" I asked.

"The executives of the oil companies. They were all trained there, and the sheikhs decided that, since these oil executives were so good at shafting the Arabs, their sons could learn how to shaft the oil companies."

"They learned well," I admitted.

"We should have sent them to the University of California at Santa Barbara, and they all would have become surfers."

"I guess it's too late to do anything about it," I said.

"Perhaps. But I think we should put an embargo on all sons of Arab sheikhs, Iranian shahs and Venezuelan presidents. When they apply to the Harvard Business School, we can turn them down by saying the class is filled, but there are openings at the University of Kentucky, where they can major in basketball. Let's not make it any tougher on ourselves in the future than we have to."

"Would the Harvard Business School go along with it?"

"If they don't, we will shut off their oil. We should shut it off anyway. Their professors got us into this mess. Let them freeze for a while and make them realize what their damn lectures did to the rest of the world."

GOOD-BYE, OLD PAINT

"Well, Old Paint, I guess it's good-bye. . . . I'll never forget you with your power steering and your disc brakes and your turbohydromatic transmission, not to mention your super-breeze air conditioning and your four-speaker AM/FM stereo radio. . . . You've been a real pal, and we've had some great times together. . . .

"Remember that time we drove on the Pennsylvania Turnpike at ninety miles an hour and the highway patrolman stopped us and asked where the fire was, and I pointed to the garbage dump which was blazing twenty feet in the air? . . . And remember when six of us decided to go to Oklahoma and you had a blowout in St. Louis during the rush hour and we stopped traffic for twenty miles both ways? . . . We had a lot of laughs, you crazy old gas guzzler you.

"I don't care what they say, you had class. You were all leather from top to bottom and your carpeting was two inches thick, and I could regulate your heat to any temperature I wanted. People used to stop and stare at your long beautiful curves, your tinted windshield and your bright silver chrome bumpers. . . . In your time, you were the most beautiful thing on the road. . . . And when your eight-cylinder multimanifold engine roared as you took off down the highway, everyone oohed and aahed in admiration. . . .

"Don't look at me that way, Old Paint. This hurts me more than it hurts you. . . . I know you're saying, 'Why me? Why, after all the beautiful rides I've given you, are you doing this?'

"You know the answer as well as I do. . . . You have a drinking problem. . . . I warned you some time ago. I said, 'Old Paint, you're consuming too much petrol, and someday it's going to catch up with you.' But you wouldn't listen. Every time we passed a gas station you had to stop in and have a few gallons for the road. I don't know how much poison you put in your tank, but I warned you eventually it would be the death of you. You laughed at me and said you could drink any car on the road under the table. You said you were built to gulp down all the superpremium they could make. You told me gas guzzling ran in the family. But you never would admit you had a problem. You never would face up to the fact that you had to consume twice as much fuel as everybody else. You pretended you were just a sociable drinker, when everyone knew you couldn't do without the stuff.

"At first, I apologized for you. I said you hung around gas stations because you needed the companionship of other cars. I said no matter how many drinks you had, you could hold your booze. But I knew I was kidding myself. I knew that if you continued on the road you were taking, you would wind up in the gutter.

"I know what you're saying. You want me to give you another chance. . . . You'll promise me that you won't drink any more gas than a Volkswagen. I'm sorry, Old Paint, but it won't work anymore. I've given you twenty or thirty chances, and you have always gone back on a gas binge as soon as I turned my back.

"I guess your riding days are over now. I tried to sell you, but nobody wanted to buy you. I couldn't even give you away. So I have no choice but to put you out of your misery. . . . It will be painless, feller. . . . And when you get to that great 'Detroit in the Sky,' there will be a gas station on every corner, where you can drink to your heart's content. . . . Good-bye, Old Paint. . . . Good-bye."

A NEW BUNDLING PLAN

Everyone came up with new methods of helping during the energy crisis. Some ideas are nutty, but others are very practical and should be called to the attention of the government.

Professor Heinrich Applebaum has been studying new methods of sharing heat and has just written a paper titled "Bundling and the Energy Crisis" which he presented to the Society of Thermostat Inspectors.

Applebaum told me after giving his report, "The place where we waste the most heat in our homes is in bed. America can no longer afford the luxury of having one person sleep in bed all by himself. If we can persuade people to voluntarily share their beds, we could turn down the thermostats in our homes seven degrees."

"Would these people have to be married?" I asked

"In normal times I would say yes. But this is the biggest emergency our country has ever faced and I think people should be given waivers if they aren't married, at least until the crisis is over."

"Then you consider bed pooling as a major solution to the heating shortage?"

"Absolutely. We must make Americans feel unpatriotic if they go to bed alone. We must instill a new spirit of bundling in this country."

"It sounds great on paper," I said, "but suppose people refuse to share their beds with others?"

Applebaum pursed his lips. "Then the government will have to step in and take forceful measures. These could include putting a surtax on citizens who insist on sleeping alone. This tax would be so high that it would be very unprofitable to refuse to bundle with somebody else. We could also give tax deductions to those who are willing to pool their beds. For example, if Bob and Carol and Ted and Alice were willing to bundle together, they would get ten percent off on their income taxes."

"What about people who *have* to sleep alone, such as policemen, doctors and newspaper reporters?"

"They would have a special sticker put on their beds exempting them from the bundling laws. This sticker would be given only to people who could prove their work is so essential they cannot bundle up with anybody."

"How do you think the American people will take to forced bundling?"

"I think the American people will be willing to share their beds with others once Nixon explains it to them. Body heat is still the greatest resource this country has, and we can get through the winter, provided everyone—and I mean everyone—cooperates with each other."

"Suppose you have a large empty bed and no one to bundle with? What do you do then?"

"We hope to set up bed-pooling information centers all over the country. All you would have to do is call a number, and we'd tell you who is looking for someone to share a bed. These centers would be open twenty-four hours a day."

"It sounds complicated," I said. "But I guess it's worth it."

Applebaum said, "It will work. To get the people to cooperate, we will have an advertising campaign on television."

"What will be your slogan?"

"Every time you share your bed this winter something in an Arab sheikh dies."

THE MEAT BOYCOTTERS

It was the fifth day of our meat boycott, and the family was sitting around the dining-room table wiping up the gravy from the cheese-and-turnip casserole that my wife had prepared for us. You could see the pride in the children's faces. They had survived almost a week without meat—and they knew they had struck a great blow for lower food prices.

"I don't even miss meat," my daughter Jennifer said.

"I don't even miss chicken," my daughter Connie agreed.

My son Joel said, "The voice of the consumer has been heard in the land."

"Then you all agree," I said, "that boycotts are the best way of showing our discontent over high prices."

Everyone agreed.

"The reason I raise the question," I said, "is that the telephone company is thinking of doubling the price of a call from ten cents to twenty cents. This would be an increase of a hundred percent and I think if they do it, we should boycott the telephone system."

The family looked at me as if I had gone mad.

"Boycott the telephone company?" Jennifer said. "But how could I talk to my friends?"

"You could write them letters," I suggested.

"No one writes anyone letters anymore," Connie said.

"Even if they did," Joel said, "they'd never be delivered."

My wife, who never knows when I'm kidding, said, "Are you serious about boycotting the phone company?"

"Dead serious," I said. "We've got to bring them to their knees. We've got to bring the cost of a telephone call down, down, down."

"I won't do it," Jennifer shouted. "I won't give up the telephone."

"You gave up meat," I said.

"Meat is just food," she shouted. "The telephone is my life."

Connie yelled, "We'd die without the telephone."

Joel agreed. "Man has to communicate by phone, or his ear will wither away."

My wife said, "I'll give up one or the other, but I won't give up both meat *and* the telephone."

"Nevertheless," I said, "if we're going to stick by our principles, we will have to boycott the telephone company, just as we will have to boycott the gasoline stations when they raise the price of gas."

"Raise the price of gas?" Joel said. "What am I going to do with my car?"

"Keep it in the garage until the gasoline companies see the error of their ways."

"How do I get to school?" Connie said.

"Take the bus."

"What's a bus?" Connie demanded.

"Don't be smart," I said. "If we're going to give up meat because they raised the prices on us, we're going to give up the telephone and gasoline, and if they raise electricity, we'll give up air conditioning."

"But we have to have air conditioning," Jennifer said.

"Look, prices are going up on everything. Why should we just sock it to the farmer? If we really want our voices heard, we've got to sock the phone company, the gasoline companies, the power companies and anyone else who thinks they can horse around with our household budget. I say we're either in the boycott business for real, or we get out of it altogether. Now what do you say?"

My wife sighed, "I'll order a pork roast from the butcher tomorrow morning."

ALL STATUS SYMBOLS ARE DEAD

Keeping up with the Joneses has been the driving force that has made Americans the big spenders of all time. In our neighborhood we always did what the Joneses did, and sometimes it almost killed us. But that's what America was all about—or at least that was what America was all about until the energy crisis.

During that time Jones was informed that his brand-new Lincoln Continental was no longer a status symbol.

The person who informed him was Plotkin, a nonconformist in our neighborhood who drives a 1970 Toyota.

I must say Plotkin was rather cruel about it.

"You're finished, Jones!" Plotkin screamed in front of Jones' house. "No one is going to keep up with you anymore."

A small group of neighbors awakened by the noise gathered on the sidewalk.

"Hush, Plotkin," a lady said. "You're ruining the neighborhood."

"I'm not ruining the neighborhood," Plotkin shouted back.

"Jones is ruining the neighborhood with that fuel-eating monster. You want to keep up with Jones, go ahead. But when you run out of gas in three blocks, don't come crying to me."

"Plotkin," I said, "why are you making such a scene over Jones' automobile?"

"Because for years I've suffered by not keeping up with the Joneses. All of you considered me a freak because I drove a Toyota. Don't think I didn't know what you said to your kids: 'If you don't study in school, you'll end up like Plotkin getting twenty-five miles to the gallon.'"

"We never said that, Plotkin," I protested.

"Jones said it," he replied. "His children used to taunt my children with stuff like 'I hear your father has to roll down his car windows by hand.' At PTA meetings whenever I got to say something, Jones would sneer, 'Sit down, Plotkin. What could a man who doesn't have power steering know about education?'"

"Be generous, Plotkin," I begged. "With an energy crisis we all have to love each other."

"Not me. All you social climbers in this neighborhood who kept up with the Joneses have no right to tell me to be generous. Why, you wouldn't even park next to me at parties. My Toyota was a pariah. And Jones was the leader of the band. Come out, Jones, and I'll drive you around the block in a car that will still be on the road a year from now."

"Will you stop shouting?" someone asked. "Can't you imagine how upset Jones must be?"

"Tough luck," Plotkin said. "Jones is finished for good. If you want to get through the energy crisis, you will have to forget he was ever born."

"He's right," Mrs. McTavish said. "If we hadn't kept up with Jones, we wouldn't be caught in a gas squeeze now."

"Jones was the one who made us afraid to buy a small car," Blimpington said.

I was caught up in the recrimination. "Come out of the house, Jones, you lousy, materialist ratfink! What are we going to do with the cars we bought to keep up with you?"

Plotkin tooted on the horn of his Toyota as the rest of us started throwing rocks at the Joneses' house.

Jones never did come out of his house, but it didn't make any difference. Everyone in our neighborhood is now keeping up with the Plotkins, which is what we should have been doing all along.

THE PRESIDENT FLIES COMMERCIAL

Almost everyone in Washington was greatly impressed with President Nixon's sacrifice in flying commercial to San Clemente, California, for the holidays. In taking a United Air Lines flight, the White House pointed out, the President was setting an example for saving fuel and also showing his faith in the commercial aviation industry.

But there are a few people in the town who are concerned the President might make a habit of flying on a commercial airline, and it could endanger the national security of the country.

Suppose, for example, the President gets a call at San Clemente from Henry Kissinger in Washington, D.C.

"Mr. President, I think you better get back right away. The Russians are up to something in the Middle East, and it could mean very serious consequences for the free world as we know it."

The President shouts to his wife, "Pat, we have to get back to Washington right away! Tell Tricia and the Secret Service to pack immediately. We're leaving in a half hour."

Mr. Nixon dials the airline. He gets a recording.

"Due to the energy crisis," the voice says, "all of our reservation clerks are tied up. Your call has been put into a computer, and as soon as one of them is free, we will connect you.

"Please do not hang up as this will be the last voice you hear until someone is free to serve you."

The President holds for forty-five minutes. Finally he gives up and says to the family, "Come on, we'll go to the airport and get our reservations there."

The party of twenty jumps into the limousines and drives to the Los Angeles airport. "You get the luggage," the President yells to Pat. "I'll get the tickets."

Mr. Nixon gets into a long line. He waits twenty minutes and finally gets up to the counter. Just as he's about to say something, the reservation clerk puts up a sign: NEXT COUNTER PLEASE.

The President says, "Look I've got to get to Washington, D.C."

The clerk who is counting his cash says, "I don't care if you're the President of the United States. This counter is closed."

"But I am the President of the United States."

"You are? Could I have your autograph?"

"Yes," the President says, signing his name. "Now can I have tickets to Washington, D.C.?"

"I'm sorry," the clerk replies. "I'm going to lunch."

The President gets in the next line. Pat comes up and says, "You should have gotten in *this* line in the first place."

The President, trying to hold his temper, says, "Pat, I don't need you to tell me which line I should have gotten into. Now shut up."

Pat, in tears, says, "You never talked to me that way when we flew on Air Force One."

A half hour later the President is at the counter. "I would like twenty first-class seats to Washington, D.C., on Flight 151."

The reservation clerk goes to the computer and starts hitting the keys.

"We don't have twenty first-class seats. We can put three in first class, twelve in tourist, and the rest will have to be standby."

"All right, but hurry," the President urges. "The plane is leaving in five minutes."

"Is this family plan?" the reservation clerk asks.

"Three on family plan; the Secret Service men will fly tourist."

"How old are they?"

"What do you mean how old are they?"

"If they're under twenty-one and have student cards, they can fly for twenty-five percent off."

"For heaven's sakes, please, I don't want to miss the plane. A generation of peace depends on me getting on this flight."

"Yes, sir. I'll have to write up these tickets."

"Look, just take this money and write them up later."

"I'm sorry, sir. That would be highly irregular. You do have time, you know."

"What do you mean I have time?"

"Flight 151 has been canceled. The next flight will leave at nine o'clock tonight with a change of equipment in Waco, Texas."

THE OIL AUCTION

Not long ago it was announced in Tehran that an oil auction was held and the oil was sold for a record price of $17 a barrel.

Not many years ago that was what a barrel of wine was selling for. It occurred to me that if the price of oil kept rising, oil auctioneers would soon describe their product with the same intensity that wine auctioneers use when selling theirs.

"Ladies and gentlemen, today we are auctioning off the greatest barrels of oil produced in the Middle East. They are the 1973, 1974 and 1975 crop, which, as all of you know, were vintage years for Middle East oil. The conditions were perfect, with plenty of sunlight, sandy soil and just enough rain to give the oil a nice, clean, fresh aroma.

"Our first offering comes from the estate of Sheikh Abu Dhabi. What am I bid for this priceless barrel? As you know, the Château Abu Dhabi oil is the sweetest in all of Kuwait, with not a trace of sulfur. It can be served with Cadillacs, Mercedes Benzes, Lincolns and Rolls-Royces. This is a *premier grand cru.* Do I hear a hundred? . . . Do I hear two hundred? . . . Do I hear three hundred? . . . Three hundred once, three hundred twice . . . three hundred three times. . . . Sold to the Japanese gentleman waving frantically in the back.

"The next selection comes from the property of the Sheikh of Bahrein. As you know, the sheikh labels his own oil right at his private refinery.

"It is prized by oil connoisseurs all over the world for its deep-black coloring and its soft and supple flavor. You will not find anything smoother to put into a generator or a truck. May we begin the bidding. Three twenty . . . four hundred

. . . four fifty? Do I hear any higher than four fifty? . . .
Sold to the Frenchman in the first row.

"Now, ladies and gentlemen, I have a surprise for you.
This barrel that my associates are bringing onto the stage is a
1973 Côte de Faisal. Yes, ladies and gentlemen, the legendary
Arabian champagne of oil. This bubbly liquid, which once
greased only the palms of American oil companies, is now
made available to anyone who renounces his ties with Israel. I
shall start the bidding at five hundred a barrel. Five
fifty . . . six hundred . . . six fifty. . . . Ladies and gentlemen, may I remind you that once the Côte de Faisal is
consumed there may never be any more . . . seven fifty
. . . eight   hundred. . . .   Once . . . twice . . . three
times. . . . Sold to the two English gentlemen fighting with
their umbrellas on the stage.

"The last stock does not come from a noted oil property,
but I believe you will be amused by its pretensions.

"It comes from the wells of an unassuming tribal chief in
the north of Iraq. It is called Château Haut-Bedouin and while
it does not have the prestige of a Château Glowy or Côte de
Faisal, it is superb everyday oil that would be most welcome
in a Volkswagen, Datsun, Dart or Pinto.

"Please do not be fooled by its color. Although a dark
brown while it remains in the barrel, it will turn black when
burned at room temperature.

"What am I bid for this noble fuel? Do I hear two
hundred . . . four hundred . . . six hundred? . . . Do I
hear eight hundred? . . . One thousand from the German
gentleman . . . two thousand from the Swiss banker . . .
ten thousand . . . ten thousand once, ten thousand twice, do
I hear any more? . . . Sold to Richard Burton for ten
thousand . . . What's that? Certainly we'll gift-wrap it for
you, Mr. Burton. And our best to your lovely wife."

A MILE FOR A CAMEL

The French made a new deal with Saudi Arabia—oil in
exchange for Mirage airplanes and sophisticated arms. The
British are in the process of making a similar deal with other

Arab oil-producing countries including the tiny sheikhdoms along the Persian Gulf.

The cruel fact is that in order to guarantee an adequate fuel supply for itself, an industrialized nation is now willing to give the Arabs all the weapons they want.

The big question is how much sophisticated armaments can the oil-producing Arab states absorb? Most of their land is covered with sand inhabited by Bedouins who still are not quite used to the sudden wealth that is being showered on them.

The following scene will probably take place in a year or two:

A Bedouin camp 300 miles from the Saudi Arabian capital of Riyadh. The chief of the area pulls up in a brand-new British armored personnel carrier.

"Ahmed," shouts the chief, "you lazy lout, wake up and come out of your tent. I have a gift from the king for you!"

Ahmed rushes out of the tent. "Did you bring me a camel?"

"I did better than that, my desert friend. See what I have on the back of the new British armored personnel carrier?"

Ahmed follows him to the rear of the truck.

The chief strips off the canvas from the object he has in tow.

"What is it?" Ahmed asks, staring at the strange machine.

"It is the latest French fighter plane, the Phantom-Mirage. It will fly at speeds over eleven hundred miles an hour and can carry six air-to-air supersonic missiles. Now what do you say?"

"I still would rather have a camel," Ahmed replies.

"How dare you talk that way about a gift from your most gracious sovereign?"

"Forgive me," Ahmed says fearfully, "but I already have four British fighters, six American Sky Hawks and seven heavy armored helicopters out behind my tent. What I really need is something that can cross the desert and doesn't use up water."

"I will forget I heard your treasonous words. His majesty has vowed that every citizen in his country will have a complete air squadron of his own by 1977. Now where do you want us to put the Mirage?"

"Put it next to the British Centaur tanks you brought me last week. Are you sure I was supposed to get thirty tanks? You know we don't have any children."

The chief checked in his book. "That's correct. You are to have thirty tanks, plus two thousand rounds of armor-piercing cannon shells."

"Are you certain his majesty didn't mention anything about giving me a camel? You see my old one is on his last legs, and if I could get a new camel, I could sell the dates from the Wadi Oasis and go to the market at Medina and—"

"Silence, you ungrateful wretch. The next thing you will tell me is that you don't want a nuclear submarine."

"A nuclear submarine?"

"That is right. The French have agreed to sell us one thousand nuclear submarines in exchange for one thousand barrels of oil. As soon as we get the transportation, we will be delivering one to you."

Ahmed sighs. "All right. But if you can't get me a camel, what about a donkey? I could make do with a donkey until I have enough money to buy a camel."

The chief got back on his armored personnel carrier and just laughed. "What industrialized country in the world would give us a donkey?"

DANGERS OF CAR POOLING

The problem with car pooling is when you have four people sharing a vehicle, tensions arise that can cause great emotional damage to all those concerned. To deal with the situation, many cities are setting up car-pool clinics where car poolers can get counseling and help.

I attended one in Fairfax, Virginia, the other evening. The car-pool counselor, a Mr. Sims, was seated in a comfortable chair smoking a pipe. Four men in business suits sat nervously in a semicircle around him. They refused to look at each other.

Mr. Sims said, "The important thing in this session,

gentlemen, is to let it all hang out. What seems to be the problem?''

One of the men spoke up. ''Arthur's the problem.''

''Could you be more specific?'' Sims asked.

''As soon as he gets in the car, he starts singing 'Oh, What a Beautiful Morning.' Even when it's raining. I can't stand a cheerful person at that hour.''

Arthur spoke up. ''Well, I like to sing in the morning. It sets me up for the day. Harold gets in the car and just reads his newspaper and doesn't even say hello to anybody. What kind of car pool can you have if someone doesn't even know you're there?''

''Oh, yeah,'' Harold replied. ''The reason I put my nose in my newspaper is I can't stand the way Sidney drives. He zooms in and out of traffic, cursing every driver on the road. My ten-year-old son could do a better job of getting us to work.''

Sidney went red. ''At least I don't smoke those smelly cigars in the morning. And while we're saying what's on our minds, I've never seen you use the car ashtray once.''

Harold responded, ''I don't use your ashtrays because they're always full of cigarette butts. It's not fun to see a filthy ashtray at breakfast time.''

Mr. Sims turned to the fourth man who hadn't said anything. ''Alistair, you're very quiet. Is there anything you'd like to get off your chest?''

''Yes, there is,'' Alistair said. ''Everyone in the car pool forgot my birthday.''

Arthur moaned, ''Oh, for God's sake.''

''Well, it may not be important to you, but my birthday means a lot to me. I didn't expect a cake or anything like that. But what would it have cost you all to say, 'Happy Birthday, Alistair'?''

''It slipped our minds,'' Harold replied. ''If it will do anything for you, happy birthday.''

''It's too late,'' Alistair sulked. ''I remembered your birthday, Harold.''

''So we forgot,'' Sidney said. ''We had other things to think about.''

Alistair wouldn't budge. "Car poolers are supposed to remember each other's birthdays."

Mr. Sims said, "I perceive tremendous tension in this pool. Now the question is what do we do about it?"

"I want out," Arthur said. "If I can't sing 'Oh, What a Beautiful Morning,' I would just as soon take the bus."

"I'm for going our separate ways," Harold said.

"Now, wait a minute," Mr. Sims said. "Car pooling is a very serious institution. When you take a vow to share an automobile with another person, you promise to love, honor and cherish him in sickness and in health. All of you have to make more of an effort to understand each other and live with each other two hours a day.

"Car pooling isn't like marriage, something that you can treat lightly. Remember, what the energy crisis has joined together let no man cast asunder. And keep this in mind: If you break up your car pool and join another one, you'll probably wind up with the same kind of people you left behind."

WOMEN'S LIB AND GAS

I dropped over to Pettigrew's house at six o'clock one night, and much to my surprise, I found him setting the table.

"Pettigrew," I said in astonishment, "what on earth are you doing?"

"I'm setting the table."

"But that's women's work."

"You're wrong," he said. "Clara and I have worked out a new arrangement which I must admit was brought about by Women's Lib."

"What do you mean?"

"We've divided the duties at home. I now set the table."

"What does she do?"

"She finds gas for the car."

"You've got to be kidding."

"I'm not kidding. As you recall," he said, mixing us drinks,

"Clara's been very unhappy for the past year. The children are in school, and she was complaining bitterly that she didn't have enough to do and that she found herself unfulfilled. I must admit it was a tough time for us.

"But then the energy crisis happened, and I said to her, 'You've been wanting to do something with your life to prove you are your own person. Why don't you go out and find some gas?'

"At first she thought she was unqualified to do something as complicated as that, but I persuaded her that she could do anything she set her mind to. After all, she had four years of college and had worked before she got married. I assured her after a few weeks she would get the hang of finding gasoline. Then instead of just being Mrs. Irving Pettigrew, wife of the vice-president of the No-Fault Insurance Company (NFIC), she would become Clara Pettigrew whose profession was finding petrol for our car."

"And she agreed to do it?"

"Yes, she did. At first it was rather tough. She would come home with a quarter tank or a half tank or sometimes a dollar fifty's worth and she was very discouraged. But I never criticized her because I knew she needed building up. I said, 'Clara, for a beginner you're doing swell. I know some wives who have been at it twice as long as you have and sometimes they don't even come home with a dollar's worth of gas a day. Now tomorrow you go out real early, like, say, seven o'clock, and get a good spot in line and you should be able to get the tank filled by three in the afternoon.' "

"And did she get the tank filled?"

"Not exactly. By the time she got to the pump they had run out. But she did manage to buy four gallons in Rockville at six that night, so the day wasn't a complete loss."

"I must say," I said, as Pettigrew mixed me another drink, "I never thought Clara could go back to work after all those years as a housewife."

"I'm very proud of her. She takes getting gas for us very seriously. Many mornings she's gone before I wake up and arrives home after I've taken my shower in the evening. She's got every gas station in town pinpointed, and she methodically goes from one to another—a dollar's worth here and a dollar's worth there. I tell you when I see the look of satisfaction on her face in the evening after she has managed to get almost a full tank, I don't mind pitching in and setting the table at all."

"And it's saved your marriage?"

"I've never seen Clara happier. She feels for the first time she's needed and she finally has a challenge worthy of her talent. In the evenings we have something to talk about together, and the beauty of it is that she gets the tank filled on her own. No one even knows she's Mrs. Irving Pettigrew."

"I'm happy for both of you. Where's Clara now?"

"She's in line at an Amoco station in Gaithersburg and just called to say she'd be a little late for dinner."

THOSE WERE THE DAYS

Everyone seems to agree that the United States is going through a nostalgia craze. What people are not aware of is that the nostalgia gap, which used to be ten to twenty years, is closing fast, and now people talk about the good old days of a year or six months ago.

Cyrus Wankel, who runs a nostalgia store here in Georgetown, says that the biggest nostalgia items in his store are less than twelve months old.

"I guess the energy crisis is responsible," he said. "People talk about the good old days, and they want something to remind them of the past. For example, here is some Tupperware. Remember when you used to get a plate every time you bought five gallons of gasoline? And here are some green stamps. It's hard for people to imagine the days when they got green stamps just for driving into a gas station."

"Those were great times," I said, wiping a tear from my eye.

"Here are some ashtrays with Spiro Agnew's photograph on them."

"Who?"

"Spiro Agnew. He was the thirty-ninth Vice President of the United States."

"Under whom?"

"Richard M. Nixon."

"Oh, yeah. I think I remember."

"Some of our biggest sellers are these Cadillac, Lincoln and Chrysler full-page advertisements that promoted the largest, most comfortable cars on the road."

"What do people do with them?"

"They frame them and hang them on the wall. They make lovely decorations and bring back fond memories of an era we'll never see again."

"What are these photographs?" I asked.

"They're pictures of different people who appeared in front of the Watergate Committee in 1973."

"I think I remember the hearings. The faces look familiar, but I can't place the names."

"That's why the photos sell so well. No one can remember any of the witnesses, but they associate them with a past that was so much happier and simpler than it is today."

"What are these Earth Day bumper stickers?"

"Well, a few years back environment was a big thing in this country, and everyone talked about it. People used to put Earth Day stickers on their cars and hold rallies demanding clean air and water. It was quite a fad. Now the only people who are interested in environment are collectors."

"I hate to show my ignorance, but I see these Richard Kleindienst match covers. Who was Richard Kleindienst?"

"Wait a minute, I'll look it up in the Nostalgia History Catalogue," Wankel said. "Here it is, Richard Kleindienst was Attorney General under Nixon, after John Mitchell and before Elliot Richardson and William Saxbe. He didn't last very long, so he didn't have many match covers made."

"That political poster over there is interesting. It says 'Taxpayers for Nixon' and it's signed 'The Committee for the Re-Election of the President.'"

"People buy them as gags," Wankel said.

I walked down the aisle and saw a glass case. Inside were cuts of sirloins, filet mignons and T-bone steaks with 1972 prices on them. My mouth watered.

"How much are these?" I asked Wankel.

"That's my private nostalgia collection of meat," he said. "It's not for sale."

WAITING FOR GAS

People were hard put as to what to do while waiting in line for gasoline. After reading *The Winds of War* from cover to cover, they still had several hours to kill before they could get near a pump.

As a public service we present a few things drivers could do to while away the time.

The first is the "license plate game." Add up all the numbers on the license plate directly in front of you. Then multiply by 10. Divide this figure by 2, and you should get the price of what a roast beef will cost you when you stop off at the supermarket on the way home.

Count the number of small foreign cars that drive past you going in the opposite direction while you are waiting for gas. If you can get to the station before the figure reaches 500, you've won the game.

Start a pool with the other drivers in the line. Each person guesses how much gas in dollars the attendant will allow each driver to buy. The one who comes closest to the right amount wins all the money in the pool.

Enroll in a college correspondence course, and do all the work in your automobile. We know one lady who started as a freshman in biology and won her master's degree before she got to the pump.

Many people have wanted to take up painting as a hobby but were never able to find the time. Buy some paints and several canvases and set up an easel in your car. It is quite possible that by the time you get your tank filled you will have enough pictures to hold an exhibition.

Make jewelry in the front seat. This is one of the most relaxing ways of killing the hours. You can put the finished products on the hood and sell them to other drivers waiting to get near the station as well as passersby who are looking for bargains. A note of warning: You should have a vendor's license if you're going to sell anything on your hood. If you see a policeman coming, stash all the jewelry in your trunk.

This next idea requires a little investment, but the returns could be great. Have a telephone installed in the dashboard, and start selling the *Encyclopaedia Britannica* by phone. One lady we know made $600 in commissions and never moved more than four blocks.

Hold your bridge games in your car. If it is your turn to be the hostess, invite three friends to go down to the gas station with you. Set up a board between the front seat and the back. You'd be surprised how fast the day goes when you're playing cards. One word of caution: Do not change partners while the vehicle is moving.

For those who need to vent their frustrations while waiting for gas, I might suggest making up a dart board with all the oil companies in the circles and King Faisal's photograph in the bull's-eye. Put the board in your rear window, and try to toss the darts over your shoulder.

This final idea is for housewives. Use the time in line to have an affair with someone who really loves you for yourself and not because you're an odd or even number.

Tell your lover which gas station you will be waiting at. The beauty of having an affair while waiting for petrol is that you will have all the time in the world to spend with your paramour, and no one will suspect either of you of being anything but a nice couple in an embrace while waiting for a few gallons of fuel.

Even if your husband finds out about the affair, he won't be too upset as long as you bring home a full tank of gas.

FASTEN YOUR BELT

If President Nixon is really serious in his campaign to protect Americans from invasion of privacy, he might start with the 1974 automobile safety belts. These harnesses which are attached to screaming buzzers on the dashboard may save lives, but they're also wrecking marriages, driving people stark raving mad and causing untold havoc on the road.

Just the other day I was in Tucson, Arizona, and the Sheltons offered to take me to dinner in their new 1974 station wagon. There were six of us in the car, three in the front seat and three in the back. Everyone was in a jovial mood.

Then Shelton tried to start the car. A red light the size of a highway billboard lit up, and a buzzer which sounded like an air-raid siren went off.

Shelton yelled to his wife, "Fasten your safety belt!"

"It is fastened!" she screamed back over the din.

"Well, it isn't fastened right. Put the shoulder strap over your chest."

"It is over my chest," she said angrily. I was sitting between them in the middle seat.

"Maybe it's my belt!" I yelled. I unhooked and then rehooked the belt, but the buzzer wouldn't stop.

"Hurry up," someone in the back seat shouted, "or the whole car will self-destruct!"

Shelton leaned over me, grabbed his wife's shoulder harness and pulled it tightly around her.

The red light went off and the buzzing stopped.

"There," said Shelton, "that's better."

"I'm choking," Mrs. Shelton gasped. "I can't breathe."

"Don't do anything," Shelton cried, "or the buzzing will start again."

"I can only hold my breath for two minutes," Mrs. Shelton gagged.

I lifted the shoulder harness from her neck, and the red light went on again and the scream of the buzzer filled the car.

Shelton hit the wheel with both his hands. "I told you not to touch her belt."

"But her face was all green," I said.

"Everybody get out," Shelton said. "Let's see if I can solve this thing."

We all got out of the car. Shelton studied the front seat.

"All right, my harness goes in this slot, your harness in this slot and her harness goes in this one. Now let's all get back in the car again, and I don't want to hear any buzzers."

We got back in and in five minutes managed to get the harnesses around us.

Shelton turned on the ignition and everything on the dashboard flashed red.

"You hold her harness," Shelton yelled to me, "and let her hold yours!"

"Who's going to hold yours?" I shouted.

"I'll hold my own."

"How are you going to drive?" I asked him.

"Who cares, as long as I can stop the buzzing?"

I was holding onto Mrs. Shelton's harness for dear life, and she had my seat belt in the crook of her elbow. Shelton had one hand underneath his seat and was driving with the other.

For five minutes it was quiet in the car. Then Mrs. Shelton said, "I think the circulation in my arm has been cut off. There's no feeling in it."

"We've only got three miles to go," Shelton raged. "Hang on."

"Please let go of my harness," Mrs. Shelton begged me.

"If you do, I'll kill you," Shelton said to me.

We made it to the restaurant just before Mrs. Shelton passed out.

It was a good dinner, but no one really cared. Everyone was thinking of the drive back to the hotel.

USE LESS, PAY MORE

I went into Burberry's house one night, and much to my surprise, I found every light in his house on.

"Burberry, have you taken leave of your senses?" I said. "Don't you know there is an energy crisis?"

Burberry plugged in the toaster, the coffeemaker and the iron. "I know it," he replied. "And I'm trying to do something about it."

"By turning on all the lights and using all these electric gadgets?"

"That's right," he said, turning up the thermostat to 80. "You see, the electric companies say they can't make any money if we conserve electricity. The only way we can bring prices down is if electric usage goes up."

"You're putting me on."

"I'm not putting you on," he said, plugging in his wife's hair dryer. "A few months ago the President and George C. Scott went on the air, separately of course, and said we had to conserve energy if we were going to be able to maintain our great way of life. So everyone cut down on using electricity.

We turned off our lights, cut down our thermostats and reduced the use of all our electric appliances. They estimated the American people saved between ten percent and twenty percent during the winter. Everyone thought if he conserved, he would at least save money on his electricity bills.

"Well, it turned out just the opposite. The electric companies all asked for rate increases because people weren't using enough of their product. It turns out they all want to be paid for electricity we haven't used."

"But that doesn't make sense," I said.

"What the hell does make sense about the energy crisis?" Burberry said. "My family froze their butts off this winter as a patriotic gesture, and now we find the electric companies want to put a surcharge on them."

"On your butts?"

"No, not on our butts, on our conservation methods.

"The electric companies are the only ones who want to charge you more for using less electricity. I cut down on smoking last year. The cigarette companies didn't send me a letter saying because I cut down on smoking they would have to charge me more a pack. We gave up high-priced steaks. My butcher didn't send me a bill for not eating steaks. Why should the electric companies send me a letter saying because I didn't use enough electricity I'm going to have to pay more for it?"

"I guess if they don't sell enough electricity to their customers, they lose money on it."

"Okay, so that means if I use more electricity, they'll make money and then be able to charge me less."

He yelled into the kitchen. "Honey, did you put the stove and oven on?"

"Burberry," I said, "I know what you say is true, but I think you've missed the point. Everyone is expected to make sacrifices during an energy crisis. I'm not talking about real sacrifices. What could be a greater sacrifice for an American than to use less electricity but at the same time compensate the electric companies by paying more for it? That's what George C. Scott and President Nixon were talking about when they asked you to turn your lights out."

By this time Burberry had turned on his vacuum cleaner,

and I didn't hear his reply. But as an accomplished lip reader, I was just as glad I couldn't.

FAREWELL TO THE ENERGY CRISIS

Three moving men walked into the office of the Energy Crisis and started taking down the pictures and the graphs.

"What are you guys doing?" the Energy Crisis asked.

"We have orders to move all your stuff out. They're moving another crisis into this office."

"But I just got here," the Energy Crisis protested.

"Don't talk to us. We just do what they tell us."

The Energy Crisis ran across the street to the White House.

"I'm the Energy Crisis," he told the guard at the gate, "and I have to see the President right away."

The guard telephones the President's office: "Rose Mary, I have some nut out here who says he's the Energy Crisis and he has to see the President. . . . That's what I thought."

The guard said, "The President can't see you, and his secretary says if you have any problems to take them up with his counselor for National Crises in the Executive Office Building. Here's a pass. Give it back to me when you come out."

The Energy Crisis went to the office written on the pass. He was kept waiting for two hours. Finally, the secretary said he could go in.

The counselor hardly looked up. "Sit down and make it short," he said.

"Why am I being moved out of my office?" the Energy Crisis demanded.

"You want it straight? We don't need you anymore. You're washed up. Get lost."

"But only a few months ago the President said I was the most important issue of the decade. He said I would be here through the eighties. I moved my family to Washington. I gave up a good job with Consolidated Edison and a pension. How can you suddenly decide I'm not needed anymore?"

The counselor said, "You served a purpose. You took

people's minds off other crises. But we can't keep you around forever. The American people don't like you, and you're going to have to be sacrificed for political expediency.''

"But don't you understand? Nothing's changed. We're going to run out of oil and fossil fuels if we don't have a strong conservation program. Look, I've worked out a plan—''

"We're not interested in your plans. If we run out of gas, we run out of gas, but there is no sense worrying everybody about it. Why don't you just admit you don't have what it takes to be a good crisis and leave quietly?''

"What about the Arabs? Suppose they put their boycott on again? Then where are you?''

The counselor yawned. "You really are a bore. Can't you get it through your head this country will not stand for an Energy Crisis? When people had to wait in line for gasoline, we almost had a revolution on our hands. We have a tough election coming up this fall in Congress, and if you were still around in November, we could lose everything. You're nothing but bad news.''

"But don't you see what you're doing to me? A lot of people didn't believe in me in the first place. They said I was a fraud. They said you brought me in just so the oil companies could raise their prices. If you kick me out now, no one is ever going to believe me again.''

"Look,'' the counselor said, "you're too caught up in your own problems. You have to see the big picture. We have crises coming out of our ears. We have Watergate, we have tax problems, and we have a credibility gap on our hands. We don't have any room for you. As a matter of fact, we need your office for the lawyers who will be working on the President's impeachment.''

"I still think you're making a mistake,'' the Energy Crisis said.

The counselor replied coldly, "We know what we're doing, or we wouldn't be in the White House. Oh, by the way, the President asked me to give you this set of cuff links with his seal on it to show his gratitude for all you did for him. I guess that's all. Now if I could just have your key to the men's room.''

X. THE CHERRY TREE CAPER

"EXPLETIVE DELETED"

On October 13, 1960, John F. Kennedy debated Richard Nixon on television. At the time, the question of Harry Truman's cussing came up. Mr. Kennedy refused to apologize for Mr. Truman's salty language, but Mr. Nixon had strong feelings that a President of the United States should not curse.

He said in part, "One thing I have noted as I have traveled around the country is the tremendous number of children who come out to see the Presidential candidates. I see mothers holding up their babies so they can see a man who might be President of the United States. I know Senator Kennedy sees them, too. It makes you realize that whoever is President is going to be a man that all children of America look up to or look down on, and I can only say I am very proud that President Eisenhower restored dignity and decency and, frankly, good language to the conduct of the Presidency of the United States.

"And I only hope, should I win this election, that I could approach President Eisenhower in maintaining the dignity of the office and see to it that whenever any mother or father talks to his child, he can look at the man in the White House and, whatever he may think of his policies, he will say 'Well, there is a man who maintains the kind of standards personally that I would want my child to follow.' "

I must admit that even though it's been fourteen years since Mr. Nixon said this, I was very moved. Perhaps, I thought, for the first time in history this country would have a President who didn't cuss.

Although Mr. Nixon didn't make it in 1960, he did become President in 1968, and every time he drove by in the last five years I held up my son in my arms (he's now twenty) and said, "There's a President who has the kind of standards I want you to follow."

Although Joel was rather heavy, I felt it was worth the strain on my back.

You can imagine my despair and disillusionment when the transcripts of the Presidential tapes were released and it turned out Mr. Nixon might have been the cussingest President in our history. Almost every other word had an "expletive deleted," and if you count the "inaudibles" and "unclears" and "ambiguities," it's enough to make a U.S. marine top sergeant's hair stand on end.

The question is what happened between the time Nixon debated Kennedy and the time he became President of the United States.

I sincerely believe Mr. Nixon was telling the truth when he said he was shocked by Harry Truman's language. I also believe in my heart he didn't start cussing until he lost the election to Kennedy.

A friend of Mr. Nixon told me, "I never heard Dick use an 'expletive deleted' until the 1960 Illinois results of the election came in. In 1962 he lost the race for governor in California, and he let out one 'inaudible' after another. I didn't know there were that many 'expletives' in the English language. It was hard after that to have Dick over to the house when the children were around.

"I thought when he became President and he was more

secure, he'd stop using 'expletives,' but apparently once you start using them, it's hard to give them up," the friend said.

And so it turns out that President Nixon was no better than Harry Truman when it came to language, and a lot worse than President Eisenhower. It's something we'll all have to get used to.

But I know one thing—I'm no longer going to hold up my twenty-year-old son in my arms when the President drives by. Any President who promises to restore good language to the Presidency and then talks the way he did is nothing but an "inaudible" in my book.

LOWERING MORAL STANDARDS

The Environmental Morality Agency has just announced that it was lowering moral standards for the next two years.

Fosdick Fleigenheimer told me, "We feel we can lower the moral level of the country without its becoming hazardous to anyone's health."

"But why?" I protested. "The whole idea behind the Environmental Morality Agency mandate was to clean up the political pollution in the country."

"We don't like to lower the standards," Fleigenheimer said, "but we have no choice. If we raise the levels of morality in 1974, we could cause massive unemployment on Capitol Hill in November. We also feel that Congress and the administration need more time to study the best way of doing away with political pollution. I assure you the agency is still very concerned about the problem, but we do have to consider the costs."

"What about the public? They were counting on higher moral standards after Watergate."

"We've done some extensive testing in our laboratories, and we've discovered that the average American can take far more lying from his government than anyone thought he could. We know that we can increase the dose of false statements and contradictions three times the present level, and people could still live with it. While cleaning up the

Watergate atmosphere is an ideal goal, Congress and the President do not want to throw out the baby with the bath water."

"That's well put," I told Fleigenheimer. "But aren't you going to have to do something within the next two years to show the country you are sincere about instituting higher moral standards in the government?"

"I assure you we're doing everything we can within reason. The do-gooders want us to destroy the whole system in the name of morality. But it can't be done overnight. The important thing to remember is that we have been living very well with low morality levels for a long time. Some people have even thrived on them."

"Who sets the morality standards for the country?" I asked.

"The President of the United States. He is in the best position to know just how much morality the country can stand."

"But according to the transcripts, the President was shown to have very low moral standards. Isn't it dangerous to let one man have that much power?"

"Possibly. But as Father McLaughlin, who is the White House adviser, put it, 'Who wants a saint in the White House?'"

"That's true. But in 1968 President Nixon said he would clean up the political climate produced by the Democrats by 1972. Now it turns out the atmosphere is so bad you can choke on it."

"Nobody's perfect," Fleigenheimer said defensively. "If the President of the United States can live with lower moral standards, so can the rest of the country."

"Suppose Ralph Nader or John Gardner sues your agency for not carrying out the provisions of the Political Clean Air Act. What will you do then?"

"We'd have to defend ourselves. We'll tap their telephones, audit their income taxes, break into their offices and steal their doctors' records."

"That should do it," I said.

Fleigenheimer said, "You have to keep in mind political expediency in Washington must always have priority over unrealistic moral standards. Otherwise, everyone in this town would be out of a job.''

BUGGING SHOWROOMS

It was reported in the press that certain car dealers have been bugging their automobile showrooms so that they can hear what people are saying when they're out of earshot of the salesman. This, of course, makes it easier for the salesman to know what the prospective buyers are thinking, and therefore he can make a better pitch to sell a car.

Let's go into one of these showrooms. The couple has been looking at the cars on the floor alone for about twenty minutes. The salesman comes out of the back office and says, "Well, Fanny, how do you like our new Mark II Panda?"

The woman looks startled. "How did you know my name was Fanny?"

The salesman gulps. "Your husband, McKinley, told me."

The husband says, "I never told you her name was Fanny. And how did you know my first name was McKinley?"

The salesman says, "Well, honestly, I didn't know, but I took a wild guess. You *look* like a Fanny and a McKinley. Now let's talk about the car. You're in the market for a hardtop in maroon with brown leather seats."

Fanny and McKinley look at each other in astonishment.

"We are looking for that color," Fanny says. "You must be a mind reader."

"After you've been in this business as long as I have, you get to know that certain people like certain colors. Now we do have a four-door Panda in maroon with bucket seats. I'm sorry it doesn't come with a stick shift, McKinley, but you know Fanny doesn't like a stick shift, and I think you should bow to her wishes."

"I know Fanny doesn't like a stick shift and she knows she doesn't like a stick shift, but how the hell do you know she doesn't like a stick shift?"

The salesman laughs nervously. "By the way she's carrying her handbag."

"Let's get out of here," Fanny says to McKinley.

"Wait," the salesman says. "I want to be very honest with you. You two don't think you can afford a Panda, what with the orthodontist's bill for Nicky's teeth, and your daughter, Frieda, going off to Oberlin next fall, and Fanny's mother having to have that operation. Well, let me tell you. With a trade-in on your 1969 Ford Mustang, the Panda will still cost you less than five thousand dollars."

McKinley asks the salesman, "Has someone told you about us?"

"Of course not. You're perfect strangers. This is the first time I've seen you. Show me a Fanny and a McKinley who don't have a son named Nicky and a daughter named Frieda going to Oberlin in the fall!"

McKinley asks, "Can I talk to my wife alone?"

"Of course," the salesman replies and retires to the back office.

"This is a real weird place, Fanny. He knows more about us than our next-door neighbors do."

"I know," Fanny whispers. "Let's tell him we'll think it over and be back next Tuesday."

The salesman rushes out of the back office and yells, "Could you make it Wednesday? I don't work on Tuesday, and I'd hate to lose the sale."

THE CHERRY TREE CAPER

Every year we once again honor the birthday of George Washington, the first President of the United States who could not tell a lie.

Because of recent events, I got to wondering what would have happened had the young Washington cherry tree incident taken place in a Watergate-type atmosphere.

This is how the story might have gone:

When George Washington was six years old, he was given a beautiful hatchet by his father. A few days later, George's father was walking through the garden and, much to his dismay, discovered someone had cut down his favorite

English cherry tree. George's father went into a rage and sought out the guilty culprit.

He shouted for his son, but George was nowhere to be found. Then he ran into George's best friend, Ron Ziegler. "Ron," the father said, "do you know who chopped down my tree?"

Ron blanched. "I refuse to comment on a third-rate ax job of a cherry tree."

Squire Washington said, "I will get to the bottom of this if it's the last thing I do."

Squire Washington confronted his son. "George, do you know who chopped down my cherry tree?"

At first George pretended he didn't know what his father was talking about. But when Squire Washington took George by his collar and showed him the tree lying pitifully on the ground, George said, "It appears to me that some overzealous playmates of mine were involved in this shocking incident."

"Well," said Squire Washington, "I want to know who did it, so he can be punished."

"Father," said George, "while I do not condone the cutting down of this cherry tree, or any other cherry tree for that matter, I would remind you that people have been chopping down cherry trees since long before I was born."

"George, I refuse to accept the excuse that just because other people have cut down cherry trees, it is all right for someone to cut down mine. Now I'm going to ask you a question point-blank and I want an honest answer. Did you chop down this cherry tree?"

George licked his upper lip. "Father, as you know, someday I'm going to be the first President of the United States. I think it would be a serious mistake in principle for me to admit whether I did or did not cut down your tree.

"I am not thinking of myself but of future Presidents who may someday be asked by their fathers if they cut down a cherry tree. It would be breaking faith with them and would be setting a terrible precedent if I agreed to be questioned under oath about what happened to the tree."

George's father was livid. "Where is the hatchet I gave you? I want to match it with the marks on the trunk."

"I've been advised not to let you see it," George replied.

"I'll give you the licking of your life if you don't produce that hatchet!"

George went into a bush and reluctantly produced the hatchet. The father inspected it carefully. "What is this? Eighteen and one-half inches of this hatchet are missing. Where is the rest of it?"

"I think Squire Woods' little girl, Rose Mary, stepped on it."

"George, for the last time, did you chop down the cherry tree?"

"Father, I cannot tell a lie. I think we've devoted entirely too much time to the subject of your cherry tree. I've given you all the information you've asked for. I've cooperated to the fullest extent, producing everything, including my hatchet. It's time that we put this cherry tree incident behind us and got on with the business of running this plantation."

A FISHERMAN PROTESTS

At this point in time it seems to me that President Nixon and his small band of hardy defenders would be careful not to alienate any group in this country unnecessarily. The White House probably doesn't even realize it, but it has made practically every fisherman in America boiling mad.

Foster Walden, a friend and devoted angler, told me, "Every time the House Judiciary Committee asks for a piece of paper or a tape the President accuses them of going on a fishing expedition."

"What's wrong with that?"

"Nixon seems to indicate that there's something wrong with fishing."

"Come on, Foster, you're oversensitive."

"I am not," he said angrily. "Fishing, thanks to the administration, now has a dirty connotation to it. Just yesterday I told some friends at the office I was going on a fishing expedition this weekend, and they said they were going to report me to security."

"That's ridiculous, Foster. When Nixon or the White House accuses the House committee of going on a fishing expedition, they're not talking about fishing."

"What are they talking about?" he demanded.

"They're talking about the House asking for records and tapes that they have no business asking for."

"Well, why don't they just say that?"

"Because it's easier to explain it to the American people if you say they're on a fishing expedition."

"What has fishing got to do with Watergate?"

"Well, I guess the first image that comes to mind is someone sitting there holding a pole in his hand who doesn't know what he's doing."

"You see. That means if you go fishing, you're stupid," Foster said.

"Not necessarily. It could also mean you're trying to get some poor defenseless fish to bite on your hook."

"That's even worse," Foster yelled angrily. "Fishing is one of the greatest sports in the world. You don't harm anyone. You don't bother anyone. You sit there with your thoughts, and you forget all about the mess they made of everything in Washington. Why did they have to drag dirty politics into fishing?"

"I guess because the White House feels that if the American people feel the House committee is on a fishing expedition, they'll believe Congress is up to no good. After all, Foster, most people do think fishing is an asinine way to pass the time."

Foster was livid. "It is not a stupid way to pass the time, and if all those people who got messed up in Watergate had gone fishing instead of what they did, they wouldn't be in the trouble they're in today. Fishermen at least have enough sense to stay out of muck and mire."

"Those are harsh words, Foster," I said. "Look at it from Nixon's point of view. He has to use every defense he can. If he can prove Congress is just fishing, he can save himself from being impeached. After all, that's all he's got left."

"He's such a big football fan," Foster said. "Why couldn't he accuse Congress of roughing the kicker?"

"It's not the same thing. The one thing Americans understand is that fishing is a poor way to hook a President."

"Not if you use worms for bait."

Foster chuckled at his own joke.

A WATERGATE TRIVIA TEST

Watergate has been going on for so long that it is now time for the first Watergate Trivia Test.

Anyone who gets every answer right will be given executive clemency.

1. What was the name of the man who ran against Richard Nixon for President in 1972? (Since this is a tough one, we'll give you a slight hint. His first name was George, and he came from South Dakota.)

2. Nixon had two Vice Presidents during his second term in office. One was Gerald Ford. Who was the other?

3. McGovern had two Vice Presidential candidates. His first choice was Senator Thomas Eagleton. When this didn't work out, he chose someone else. What was the name of his second choice? His third choice? His fourth choice? Whom did he finally select?

4. On the night five men broke into the national headquarters of the Democratic Party at the Watergate, several men were stashed away at a motel across the street. What was the name of the motel, and how many different flavors of ice cream do they sell?

5. When Ron Ziegler was informed about the Watergate break-in, he said he would not comment on a "third-rate burglary." Name a first-rate burglary that Ziegler has commented on.

6. After the Watergate break-in, the wife of a former Attorney General claims she was held in a motel room in Newport Beach, California, against her will. How much was she charged for the two extra days?

7. What was the price of milk before the milk industry promised to donate a sizable contribution to President Nixon's Presidential reelection campaign? What was the price after they made the contribution?

8. The President has had four Attorneys General and one acting Attorney General since 1972. Which one said, "Judge us not by what we say, but by what we do"? What state was he indicted in?

9. President Nixon has insisted from the very beginning that he never had any knowledge of Watergate until March 21, 1973. What football games did he watch while the cover-up was going on?

10. Dr. Fielding, a psychiatrist in Los Angeles, had a very famous patient whom the White House was interested in. They ordered a special team called the plumbers to break into Dr. Fielding's office and steal the patient's records. But the plumbers couldn't find them. Why didn't they take Fielding's couch instead?

11. One of the major discoveries of the Senate Watergate hearings was that President Nixon taped the conversations of everyone who came into his office. When nine of the tapes were subpoenaed, the White House said only seven existed. What was the name of the man Nixon fired for failing to record the two missing conversations?

12. What two buttons on a recording machine would you have to push down at the same time you put your foot on a pedal to erase 18½ minutes of a crucial White House tape?

13. Most of the people involved in Watergate have been lawyers. What subjects did they take in law schools which made them believe that they were not doing anything wrong?

14. President Nixon's lawyers say he can only be impeached for high crimes and misdemeanors that he committed in his duties as President of the United States. Name six crimes the President could commit which have nothing to do with his government service.

15. If President Nixon is impeached, what Washington newspaper will he cancel his subscription to?

SEVEN STREAKERS

"Mr. President, you know those seven people who were arrested for streaking through the Watergate fountain last week?"

"I read about it in the newspaper, John."

"It turns out several of them worked for the White House."

"Why didn't I know about this sooner?"

"Well, Mr. President, we thought we could keep it from you. It is our belief that it would be unwise to have the President of the United States involved with streaking and all its implications."

"I am very disturbed that anyone on my staff would run nude through the Watergate fountain. Why did they do it, John?"

"They thought it would help you in the polls. The problem now, Mr. President, is that the people arrested say if we don't help them, they're going to reveal that we've been streaking in the White House for the last six months. If that gets out, we're going to be in a lot of trouble."

"That's blackmail, John. What are our options?"

"We could pay the money to them to hush them up."

"How much would it cost, John?"

"Taking into consideration their lawyers' fees and what it would cost to care for their families, I would say one million dollars."

"We could raise that easily, John. What are our other options?"

"We could say we streaked in the White House for national security reasons. We had to hire streakers because the FBI refused to streak for us, and the CIA under their mandate could streak only in a foreign country. Our streakers were hired to find out what other streakers were up to. As President it was your constitutional duty to see that the people in this country did not discard all their clothes and run around in their birthday suits."

"I see. Do we have any other options?"

"We could refuse to pay the money to the defendants and let them reveal the streaking that went on here. We could say that a few members of your staff did run nude through the halls, but no one had ever streaked through the Oval Office. As soon as you heard about it, you ordered an investigation of the streaking and insisted that those who did it had to resign!"

"What if it turns out that my closest aides were involved in the streaking, John?"

"There's that possibility, Mr. President. I saw two of the men you hold in the highest esteem run naked through Rose Mary Woods' office the other night."

"Have you ever streaked, John?"

"Yes, sir, I have, Mr. President. One afternoon, while I was working on some legislation for you, I suddenly took off all my clothes and went running on the White House lawn. The Secret Service caught me just as I was going over the fence."

"You had better go to Camp David, John, and write a full report for me."

"I'll do that, Mr. President. Now to get back to the people who were caught streaking at the Watergate. We do have another option. We could offer them executive clemency."

"How could we justify that, John?"

"We could say they were nudists on their way to sunbathe on the Potomac, and they cut through the Watergate complex to save time."

"Sure we could, John. But if I start giving executive clemency for streaking, I could lose my mandate."

"Then what should we do, Mr. President?"

"I could try to hush the whole thing up. Or I could tough it out. But I have a third option, John. Pat and I could streak down Pennsylvania Avenue tomorrow at high noon—BUT THAT, JOHN, WOULD BE WRONG."

SOME WATERGATE CRIMES

We have been warned by everyone that all the people indicted in the Watergate affair must be presumed innocent until proved guilty, and we concur.

But there are crimes they have committed for which they must be presumed guilty until proved innocent.

Here is a short list:

PURCHASING CHEAP RECORDING EQUIPMENT FOR THE PRESIDENT

This not only has caused Mr. Nixon embarrassment, but could be responsible for his downfall. By trying to save a few bucks on tape machines, the former aides to the President must take the blame not only for tapes that do not exist, but also for the erased ones that do.

SLOPPY FILING METHODS

No administration has had such messy files since Ulysses S. Grant. Every time the special prosecutor or the House Judiciary Committee lawyers ask for a relevant paper, no one seems to know where it is. This is even more tragic when you consider that everyone around the President looked so neat and clean you just assumed they would keep neat files.

BAD BOOKKEEPING

Before the Watergate scandal, everyone assumed that President Nixon was surrounded by bookkeepers. It now turns out that no one had any experience in finance, and large sums of money kept getting lost and being put in the wrong ledgers. Probably the biggest problem was that everyone was dealing in cash, which is harder to keep track of than checks.

KEEPING SECRETS

This is one of the most serious charges. As far as we know, everyone kept secrets from everybody else in the White House. No one knew what the other person was doing. President Nixon, if we are to believe him, knew nothing at all. By keeping secrets from each other, it was impossible for the staff to stick to the same story when Watergate was uncovered.

HAVING A FALSE SENSE OF SECURITY ABOUT THE FBI AND THE CIA

One of the many crimes ex-administration officials are guilty of is believing that the FBI and CIA would follow orders of the White House without questioning them. This false faith in these two institutions might have been the beginning of their undoing. The tragedy of Watergate is that the FBI and CIA could not be counted on to cover up goofs in the administration.

BELIEF IN THE MANDATE

This is not a felony, but a misdemeanor. Everyone around the President believed the election results in 1972 would guarantee that no one would be interested in how he won his mandate. Had Nixon aides not been interested in winning a mandate, there might never have been a Watergate.

OVERACHIEVING AT FUND RAISING

The success of the Nixon fund-raising drive was one of the

main reasons everything went wrong. Had the Committee for the Re-Election of the President been short of money, it never would have had the finances to get them in so much trouble. When you're broke you have no choice but to put funds into billboards and TV commercials. When you're flush, you have a tendency to hire spies and private detectives to do dirty work for you.

PLAYING TENNIS WITH EACH OTHER

The Nixon people only played tennis with each other, which kept them from knowing what the rest of the country was thinking. Had they let outsiders into their game, they might have realized that what they were plotting for the President was wrong.

WEARING THE AMERICAN FLAG PIN IN THEIR LAPELS

It is no crime to wear an American flag in your lapel. But it is a crime to believe that by wearing one, everything that you tell a grand jury automatically will be believed.

WATERGATE IS GOOD FOR YOU

Everyone from Joseph Alsop to Vice President Gerald Ford pleaded that the country should forget about Watergate so the President could devote his time and efforts to such important matters as the energy crisis.

Dr. Siegfried Siegfreed, a psychiatrist who is writing a book, *How Much Can Americans Take?*, supported the opposite view. "I think it would be more advantageous if the country could forget about the energy crisis so the President could devote his full time to Watergate."

"Why do you say that, Doctor?"

"The truth is that practically everyone in the country gets a fiendish delight reading about Watergate, while very few people get any fun reading about the energy crisis. My studies show that if you offer readers the choice of a Watergate article or one on the oil shortage, they will take the Watergate story five to one. I'm afraid that if Watergate hadn't happened, we would have had to invent it."

"But why?" I asked Dr. Siegfreed.

"Watergate is pure entertainment. It has comedy, mystery

and melodrama. I would prefer that it have a little sex as well, but we can't have everything. People identify with the Watergate characters. They are all clean-cut, short-haired Americans caught up in a soap opera which each insists was not of his making. It also involves a new element which is the question of a Presidential impeachment. The number two man has been booted out of office, and the number one man's job is on the line.

"What more escape can you offer people who are beset with inflation, unemployment and transportation problems beyond their wildest dreams?

"Without Watergate you would have a mass mental depression in this country. I maintain that Watergate is the glue that keeps the nation from falling apart.

"Take the controversy over the tapes. What a pleasure it is to see the battle being waged between the White House and the special prosecutor. What fiction writer would have had the nerve to have written the Rose Mary Woods role in the erasure of the key tape? Americans may not want to admit it, but they love every minute of Watergate. The worst mistake would be to deprive them of this marvelous farce provided them free through the courtesy of their friendly government."

"When you put it that way, Watergate does have its role in American life," I admitted.

"Show me anyone who enjoys reading about the energy crisis. Produce one soul who gets pleasure out of seeing photographs of long lines of cars at gas stations. Find me a person who gets any pleasure out of watching administration officials give daily conflicting stories on the oil situation in the country."

"I don't know of anybody," I admitted.

"When John Chancellor leads his program with a story that the cost of living went up another five percent, the country goes into the dumps. But when he starts the show by revealing the President has refused to turn over tapes and papers to Special Prosecutor Jaworski, everybody cheers up and relaxes."

"I wonder why Alsop and Ford don't appreciate the psychological value of Watergate," I said.

"I can't analyze people I haven't examined personally,"

Dr. Siegfreed replied. "But I do know that the biggest mistake this country could make would be to put Watergate behind them. As long as we can produce new evidence concerning the cover-up and high administration involvement, Americans will survive secure in the knowledge that the news can't be all bad."

LISTENING TO GOD

At a prayer breakfast here in Washington President Nixon urged Americans to join in silent prayer to determine God's will for the country.

"Too often we are a little too arrogant," he said. "We try to talk and tell Him what we want. What all of us need to do and what this nation needs to do is to pray in silence and listen to God to find out what He wants us to do."

Well, I tried it.

The other morning I was standing with my head bowed, and God said, "You're awfully quiet this morning, Arthur."

"I'm waiting for you to tell me what to do."

"That's strange, Arthur. You usually have a long list of things that you ask of me."

"President Nixon said we should stop talking, and we should listen to you and find out what you want from us."

"I don't want anything from you. I'm doing fine."

"I don't mean that, Lord. What should we, as Americans, do that would please you?"

"Well, for a start, you could clean up your air and your water."

"Oh, we're doing that. Didn't you hear President Nixon's State of the Union speech?"

"I was at a church meeting that night. It still looks pretty bad from up here."

"That's because of the energy crisis. You see, we've had to burn a lot of gook to get through the winter, and we've had to lower our environmental standards. But as soon as the crisis is over, I'm sure we'll do something about the air and water. What else can we do?"

"You seem to be having some problems down there with inflation, Arthur."

"I thought so, too. But President Nixon says everything is just great, and we're in terrific shape economically, and people have more buying power than they've ever had before."

"Hmmm, it must have escaped me. I've been getting a lot of prayers from unemployed people lately."

"That's just because of the energy crisis. Nobody wants to buy big cars."

"Then why don't they build small cars?"

"God only knows. Is there anything else you'd like to say?"

"I wouldn't have mentioned it unless you asked, but Americans seem to be violating the Ten Commandments left and right."

"Which one did you have in mind?"

"The specific one is 'Thou shall not bear false witness against thy neighbor.' "

"I imagine you're referring to Watergate now."

"You have to admit, Arthur, that someone is lying."

"It seems that way, God, but then again we don't know all the facts, do we?"

"I do."

"I forgot that. You probably do. Listen, what are the chances of impeachment?"

"Is this a prayer or a question?"

"I was just curious. It would be fun to be the first one in the country to know."

"I'd rather not comment on impeachment while the matter is now in the courts."

"What else do you want for America, God?"

"Peace, good health care, protection of the individual and an excess profits tax on the oil industry. I would also like to see the Arab oil embargo lifted before Americans really start getting mean to each other."

"You'll have to speak to Henry Kissinger about that."

"I have a call into him now, but he's out of the country."

"Is there anything else?"

"There is a lot more, but I can't talk to you now. I've got Billy Graham on the other line."

A WATERGATE CZAR

Was Watergate a hoax to take our minds off the energy crisis? Dr. Heinrich Applebaum, who keeps tabs on the Watergate industry, maintained it was not.

"The Watergate crisis is for real, in spite of what President Nixon says. In fact, it is so serious that I am advocating the only way to handle it is to appoint a Watergate czar whose functions would be similar to those of William Simon, the energy czar."

"What would he do?" I asked.

"He would make sure we would never run out of Watergate material. For example, the czar would have the power to allocate Watergate indictments so every state would get a piece of the action. At the moment, most barrels of indictments are being shipped to Washington, D.C., New York, Florida and California. The special prosecutor's office seems to be supplying only their favored customers, and this is causing extreme hardship in the Middle West, where farmers and truck drivers were depending on Watergate to get them through the winter."

"You do need a czar to straighten that one out," I conceded.

"One of the problems with the Watergate crisis is that nobody knows how many barrels of indictments the country has on hand. The only figures the administration has seen are the ones printed in the Washington *Post*. The czar would have the authority to demand from the special prosecutor's office a daily report on the number of crude indictments it has stocked up, as against the refined indictments which are ready for trial.

"Dealing with the shortage of White House tapes would also be under the czar's direction," Dr. Applebaum said. "One of the reasons for the shortage is that the President's lawyers have put an embargo on the tapes until Congress goes back to the cease-fire lines of 1972.

"Another reason," said Applebaum, "is that the President thought he had more tapes than he really did. There was a shortfall of more than one hundred tons of White House tapes, and this actually triggered the crisis. Because of new demands for the tapes from Congress and grand juries, many people believed Nixon was withholding the tapes so he could jack up the price on them."

"How would you solve that one?" I asked.

"The czar would have White House tape ration stamps printed. Each grand jury and Congressional committee would be allotted ten tapes a week. If they didn't use up their allotment, they could sell their stamps to another grand jury. This would be an equitable way of guaranteeing everyone would have enough tapes to get through the month."

Dr. Applebaum said, "The czar would also deal with the windfall profits that are being made by lawyers off the Watergate crisis. Some people have said that Watergate was created by the lawyers to double and triple their earnings in 1973 and 1974. But the lawyers have denied this and say that most of the money they have made on Watergate has been plowed back into court appeals and invested in new methods of keeping their clients out of jail.

"While this may be true, the public is very suspicious of the law industry these days, and the czar would have to recommend an excess profits tax to make sure lawyers don't benefit from Watergate at the expense of the rest of the country."

Dr. Applebaum believed although the crisis was real, there was still enough Watergate evidence in the country to implicate everyone.

"When you add up the Democratic headquarters break-in, the ITT and milk fund scandals, mass perjury by administration officials, the Howard Hughes donation, the erasure of White House tapes, the President's questionable tax returns and the impeachment proceedings, we have enough gallons of Watergate for every man, woman and child in the country, provided the czar bans all Sunday bugging."

XI. ROSE MARY'S BABY

THE MAN WHO LOST HIS TAPES

"Dick, for heaven's sake, what are you doing in those closets?"

"Dammit, Pat, I'm looking for my tapes."

"There they are."

"No, not those. I'm missing two of my favorites—John Mitchell's *Watergate Concerto* and John Dean's *Music to Be Impeached By.* They must be here somewhere."

"You're making a mess of everything, Dick. Why are they so important right now?"

"I promised them to Johnny Sirica, and he's waiting downstairs. Where the heck could they have gone?"

"Didn't you lend a bunch of tapes to Bob Haldeman a few months ago?"

"By God, I did. I'll call him. . . . Bob, this is Dick Nixon. Remember those tapes I lent you awhile back? Did you return all of them to me? Yes, I've got the Magruder *Overture to Perjury* and Colson's *Executive Clemency Symphony in D Minor.* I'm missing the *Watergate Concerto* and *Music to Be*

217

Impeached By. . . . You didn't take them? Well, look around
the house just in case. . . . Thanks. . . . By the way, how's
it going? . . . That's good to hear. . . . How am I doing?
Just great, Bob. I've never been cooler."

"Dick, maybe Tricia or Julie borrowed them."

"Tricia, Julie, come in here right away. Did either one of
you take any of my tapes?"

"No, Daddy. The last one I borrowed was the *Peace with
Honor Suite for Drums and Cymbals.*"

"I didn't touch them, Daddy. I remember David mentioning to me that you have the best tape collection of anyone in
America, and he admired the way you kept them so neatly and
in such excellent condition. He said someday he hoped to
afford equipment for his tapes like you have."

"Get the servants in here, Pat. I've got to get to the bottom
of this."

"Gracious, Dick, you seem to be making such a fuss over
two tapes when you have literally hundreds. Why don't you
just give Johnny Sirica two other tapes from your collection?"

"I promised him these two, Pat. You know Sirica. If you
promise him something and give him something else, he gets
mad."

"Well, let's think for a moment. Who else borrowed your
tapes besides Bob Haldeman?"

"There's at least a half dozen people who heard them at
one time or another. But I'm fairly certain I never lent them
the John Mitchell or John Dean tapes. They were my
particular favorites. You can't believe the sound quality I
produced from them. You can hear every note."

"Even so, Dick, they're only tapes."

"Are you crazy, Pat? They're collector's items. People
would give anything to hear those particular recordings. I'm
the only one in the country who owns them."

"Why don't you tell Johnny Sirica that you lost them?"

"I thought of that. But he won't believe me. He'll think I
don't want to give him the tapes. And then he'll get mad, and
we'll only have a big fight, and I'll lose my cool."

"Well, I don't see what else you can do, Dick. You can't
keep him waiting downstairs all day."

"Wait a minute. I just thought of something. I'll tell him the tapes don't exist. I'll tell him I never had them in the first place. I can't lend him the tapes if I don't have them, can I?"

"What will you give him instead?"

"Buzhardt's *Fantasia in A Major.*"

YOU CAN ALWAYS RECORD AGAIN

The solution to the two missing Presidential tapes is simple. The President should do them over again with the same cast. It would be no problem for the White House to rent a recording studio and hire a producer to make tapes as good as the original.

This is how it would go.

PRODUCER: Okay, Mr. President, do you have your script? Now on this tape you're getting a call from John Mitchell. It's right after Watergate and Mr. Mitchell is giving you a fill-in. Mr. Mitchell, you hold the phone over there at that mike. Are we ready? Roll 'em. This is the Nixon-Mitchell telephone conversation tape one. Go.

MITCHELL: Hi, Mr. President. John Mitchell here.

NIXON: Hello, John. How's Martha since you tied her up in Newport Beach?

PRODUCER: Cut. Mr. President, you sound too relaxed. Now you have to remember, this is right after Watergate, and it looks like the Committee for the Re-Election of the President has been involved. Could you get some anxiety in your voice?

NIXON: I never show any anxiety.

PRODUCER: Well, pretend you were just awakened or something. We want to make this thing sound real. Okay, roll it again, tape two.

MITCHELL: Do you want to start from the top or where I tell the President I can't tell him anything about Watergate because it will only upset him?

PRODUCER: All right, start from there.

MITCHELL: Mr. President, I know something you don't know.

PRESIDENT: What is it?

MITCHELL: I'm not going to tell you because you'll go through the roof.

PRESIDENT: But as President shouldn't I know everything you know? It isn't nice to keep secrets from me, John.

MITCHELL: Someday you'll thank me for not telling you about it.

PRESIDENT: Why on earth did you bring it up if you can't tell me?

MITCHELL: In the future I may have to testify that I didn't tell you about it, and I want it on the record.

PRESIDENT: Well, what did you call for then?

MITCHELL: Just to tell you I couldn't tell you anything about the Watergate break-in or who was involved.

PRESIDENT: I appreciate that. And, John, have a nice day.

PRODUCER: Beautiful. You guys were perfect. All right, let's do the second tape. Where's John Dean?

ASSISTANT: He's sitting over there being guarded by two Secret Service men. He says he doesn't want to do it.

PRODUCER: Why doesn't he want to do it?

ASSISTANT: He says he has a contract with Columbia Records, and he can't make tapes for anyone else.

PRODUCER: Get him over here to this mike.

DEAN: I can't read my script with these handcuffs on.

PRODUCER: Take off the handcuffs. Now, John, the Presidency of the entire United States is at stake. How you read these lines could affect the history of the country. Do you understand?

DEAN: I guess so. But this script doesn't sound like me.

PRODUCER: Who's going to know, John ? You're in show biz.

DEAN: The President didn't say these things to me.

PRODUCER: Look, John. Don't worry about what the President said to you. Let him worry about his own lines. Okay, let's roll. Everyone in the studio, quiet. Tape one Nixon-Dean in Oval Office alone.

PRESIDENT: I'm glad to see you, John. Do you have anything of importance to tell me?

DEAN: We need a million dollars to cover up the Watergate scandal.

PRESIDENT: But that would be dishonest.

PRODUCER: Cut. Mr. President, would you show more surprise in your voice when Dean brings up the million dollars?

SITTING ON THE TAPES

"Ron, have you seen my tapes?"

"You're sitting on them, Mr. President."

"Oh, yes, I forgot. No one is going to get these tapes, Ron. I want to make that perfectly clear."

"I know that, Mr. President. But you've been sitting on them for three days. Don't you think you ought to get some sleep? We could put the tapes in a safe."

"I'm not going to let them out of my sight. They would love to have me go to bed and leave my tapes in my safe."

"They?"

"All of *them* out there who are trying to get me. Ron, do you know they're trying to hang me with my own tapes? Well, I have a big surprise for them. I've heard these tapes, and I'm innocent. But they'll never hear them. For the rest of their lives, they'll always wonder what was on them."

"That's true, sir. But you can't keep sitting on the tapes for the rest of your administration. Why don't you give them to someone you trust to safeguard them for you?"

"Ron, I learned a long, long time ago that you can't trust *anybody*. That's why I made all these tapes. Now they can't say they told me one thing when they told me another. I've got them, Ron, and they know I've got them."

"But most of the people you bugged, Mr. President, were those who worked for you."

"What about the March of Dimes child? The Maid of Cotton? What about the Boy Scouts of America when they came to the White House? I'm sitting on it all, Ron. That's what's driving *them* nuts."

"Aren't you uncomfortable sitting on them day and night?"

"No, Ron, and do you know why? Because I'm sitting on history. When future Presidents sit on these tapes, they're going to say, 'God bless Richard Nixon for not giving them to the Watergate Senate Committee.' "

"All the same, sir, the Secret Service has assured me any time you want to give up the tapes, they will make certain that no one gets them."

"Ron, I have only nine hundred and three days as President of the United States, and do you know what I'm going to do with that time?"

"No, sir."

"I'm going to sit on these tapes."

"That's wonderful, Mr. President."

"They can threaten me. They can subpoena me. They can even impeach me, but they're not going to get one spool."

"You're a real Profile in Courage, Mr. President."

"Now I know there are some people who are going to say, 'Tricky Dick is up to his dirty tricks.' And I know there are some people who are going to ask, 'If he's innocent, why doesn't he turn the tapes over to Cox?' And I know others are going to say I doctored the tapes.

"But when I took this office in 1968, I vowed I would never do the easy thing, the popular thing, the political thing. Ron, the toughest decision I ever had to make was whether I would tape some of the people all of the time or all of the people some of the time. It was only when I talked with Butterfield that I found out I could tape all of the people all of the time. It was probably the greatest day of my life."

"You sure you don't want to go to bed, Mr. President?"

"No, Ron, I think I'll just stay here and relax with this tape of the *John Connally Concerto in F-sharp Minor.*"

BUGGING THE OVAL OFFICE

The most interesting information about President Nixon having all his offices in the White House bugged was that the tape machines were "voice activated"—that is to say, they automatically went on when someone started to talk.

Not all the conversations in the Oval Office had to do with the President and his visitors. I have in my possession a tape of two cleaning women who did not know the office was bugged. The time of the taping was 12:05 A.M.

(Sound of vacuum cleaner. Voice singing: "Carry me back to ol' Virginny." Vacuum cleaner stops.)

"Okay, Mathilde, it's my turn to be President of the United States."

"You were President last night, Clementine. It's my turn to be the President."

"I was off last night. Bethlyn must have been President last night. Now I'm going to sit in the big chair behind the desk. Who you want to be, Mathilde?"

"I'll be the queen of England."

"Don't be so smart. Why don't you be Sammy Davis, Jr.? Now come over to my side of the desk and hug me."

"I don't want to be Sammy Davis, Jr. I think I'll be Henry Kissinger."

"Okay, Henry. I want you to go to China."

"What for, Mr. President?"

"I want two orders of wonton soup, six egg rolls, a container of chop suey and a dozen fortune cookies."

"Who you want to be now, Mathilde?"

"I'll be the former Attorney General of the United States of America."

"Okay, Mr. Former Attorney General. Now I got to ask you this question. You know anything about this Watergate mess that everyone's been talking about?"

"No, sir, Mr. President. I don't know nothing about nothing, and if I did know, I wouldn't tell you."

"That's no way to talk to the President of the United States of America. I want to get to the bottom of this affair. Send in my loyal, devoted and trusted assistants."

"Who am I now?"

"You be John Dean."

"Okay, Mr. President, I am John Dean. What you want to know?"

"What's going on with this Watergate business, John?"

"You really want to know?"

"What for am I President of the United States if I didn't want to know?"

"Okay, Mr. President, I'll tell you."

"Get out of here. I don't want to know."

"Now who am I?"

"You be Haldeman."

"Hi, Mr. President. I am Bob Haldeman, your loyal and able chief administrative assistant."

"Bob, I think John Dean knows something, and he isn't telling us."

"We'll send him to Camp David and get him out of here. I never trusted him since he went on his honeymoon."

"One more thing, Bob. I need four more golf carts for San Clemente, a new volleyball court and a gazebo for Key Biscayne."

"You got them, Mr. President."

"Now you be John Connally, Mathilde."

"Yes, sir, I'm John Connally, reporting to help you out of your troubles."

"John."

"Yes, sir, Mr. President."

"Get out of here. (Laughter.)

"Well, since I'm the President, I think I'll make a proclamation. I hereby free all the slaves."

"That's President Lincoln, not President Nixon."

"I didn't say which President I was, did I?"

ROSE MARY'S BABY

One of the things the Nixon administration was noted for before Watergate was its neatness. It's hard to believe, on the basis of recent revelations, that the President has run one of the sloppiest White Houses of anyone in our history. Records get lost. Tapes don't exist. Notes are misplaced. It's not enough to impeach the President, but it certainly scares the heck out of you.

I can just see the President buzzing his private secretary, Rose Mary Woods.

"Rose Mary, get me that tough note Brezhnev sent me during the Mideast crisis."

"Yes, sir, Mr. President."

Twenty minutes later: "The note seems to be missing, Mr.

President. There's nothing in the Brezhnev folder except a telegram congratulating Princess Anne on her wedding."

"Did you look in the Princess Anne folder?"

"Yes, I did, and there is nothing in her folder except John Mitchell's resignation as Attorney General."

"Good grief, I have to get a copy of the Soviet note. Did you look in my folder?"

"Yes, I did, Mr. President. The only thing in your folder is your tough note to Brezhnev."

"Well, at least that's something. Let me see it."

"Here it is, Mr. President."

"This isn't the tough note I sent Brezhnev. It's a summary of Kissinger's talks with Golda Meir."

"Oops. Sorry about that. It was written on a shopping bag, so it was hard to decipher."

"Perhaps we could get out the tapes of my conversations with Soviet Ambassador Dobrynin. I think he summed up the Brezhnev remarks."

"I'll call the Secret Service and have them sent up right away."

A half hour later. "Mr. President, did you speak to Mr. Dobrynin on October 24 or 25?"

"Why do you ask?"

"Because the tapes marked 'Conversation with Dobrynin, Part I' seem to be a telephone call you made to Bebe Rebozo."

"Did you check the Bebe Rebozo tapes?"

"Yes, and they turned out to be a conversation you had with Emperor Haile Selassie when you were *Vice President*."

"Dammit, Rose Mary, we seem to be running a loose ship around here. Get me the tapes of my conversation with Mao Tse-tung."

"Bob Haldeman took them home with him last June."

"Well, didn't he bring them back?"

"He can't remember."

"Okay, forget the tapes. Give me the notes I dictated after my meeting with the Congressional leaders on the energy crisis."

"Here they are, Mr. President."

"Hold it. These aren't my notes on the energy crisis. They're the plays I worked out for the Washington Redskins in last year's Super Bowl game."

"Mr. President, if you don't like the way I'm doing my work, I'll be very happy to resign."

"Now, Rose Mary, stop crying. I think you're doing a wonderful job. It's just that every once in a while I can't seem to find something I'm looking for."

"You know this is not the easiest job in the world."

"Rose Mary, Rose Mary. Pat and I think the world of you. Now you just go back to your desk and forget all about the tough note Brezhnev sent me. It probably wasn't important anyway."

WHAT A HUMMER!

Dear Customer,

Congratulations! You are now the owner of a 1973 Mark VI Presidential Accident-Prone Tape Recording Machine.

The Mark VI has been scientifically developed to produce the highest-quality hums of any tape recorder on the market. It can malfunction at the press of a button, and you can erase anything you want on your tape without even knowing it.

With just a little practice you will have the greatest collection of unintelligible noises ever recorded which you can play back to friends, judges and grand juries any time you want to.

HOW TO USE YOUR MARK VI PRESIDENTIAL TAPE MACHINE

The first thing to do is sit at a desk facing your typewriter. Place your tape recorder next to you on a small table with the foot pedal underneath the desk. The telephone should be at least three feet behind your chair, almost impossible to reach.

Insert the tape into the recorder, and push the PLAY button and start transcribing the voices. Then have someone call you. As soon as the phone rings, reach back with your left hand and accidentally press the RECORD button instead of the STOP button, making certain while twisting your body to keep your left foot on the pedal.

Keep this position for 5½ minutes, which should erase 18 minutes of tape.

After you hang up the phone, put the earphones on again, release your foot from the pedal, push the PLAY button and you should hear a loud shrieking hum.

If for some reason you do not get the hum after the telephone call, you are probably doing one of several things wrong.

1. Check to see that the tape you inserted is the one you wanted wiped out. All tapes look alike and some are not worth erasing.

2. Did you by accident press the STOP button when you should have pressed the RECORD button? If you press the STOP button when the phone rings, it is IMPOSSIBLE to accidentally erase a perfectly good tape.

3. Were you sitting in the correct position when the phone rang? If the phone was not located directly behind you, it would be very difficult to reach for it and also hit the RECORD button at the same time.

4. Did you keep your foot on the pedal when you answered the phone and accidentally pressed the WRONG button? Your Presidential Tape Recorder Mark VI will not malfunction unless you push the wrong button at the right time.

5. The quality of the hum you get on your tape will depend on your foot pressure. A weak hum indicates you do not have your foot pedal pressed all the way down to the floor.

The Mark VI Presidential Tape Recorder has been tested under combat conditions. Secretaries all over the United States swear by it. Here is what Rose Mary Woods, a topflight executive secretary, says about her Presidential Tape Recorder. "I have been using the Mark VI tape machine for several months now, and I don't know how I ever managed without it. It gives me hums when I want hums, and it gives me voices when I want voices. No machine on the market can erase so much conversation so fast."

If for any reason your Mark VI fails accidentally to erase your key conversations, you may return it to company headquarters at 1600 Pennsylvania Avenue, where it will be fixed absolutely free. The life of this warranty is for three more years or impeachment, whichever comes first.

"THE EXORCIST"

When it was first revealed that 18½ minutes of a Presidential tape had been erased, General Al Haig said facetiously that it was possible that some "sinister force" was at work which no one could explain.

This became known as the "devil theory," and while it was discarded by most people at the time, it is now being reexamined in the light of the latest testimony by tape experts.

If the tape was indeed possessed by a sinister force, this means that President Nixon, or his staff, is completely innocent of destroying vital evidence.

To find out more about this, I went to visit Dr. Karras Damien at Georgetown University, who is an expert on the devil and tape recorders.

"We have had many cases of the devil possessing Sony recording machines," Dr. Damien said. "But this is the first time I've heard of the devil getting into a Uher 5000."

"How do you know it's the devil?" I asked.

"Who else would want to erase eighteen and a half minutes of tape? Certainly not the President or Rose Mary Woods or anyone else associated with the Watergate investigation. The only one to gain on something like this is Satan."

"I don't understand why the devil would get mixed up in Watergate."

"The devil's job is to make trouble and raise doubts and plant suspicion. He knew the best way to do this was to get inside the Uher 5000 and wipe out portions of the tape that were vital to proving the President's innocence."

"Are you trying to tell me the buzz we heard on the tape was the devil?"

"I am. We know from our research when Satan is up to mischief, he always buzzes for exactly eighteen and a half minutes."

"Then why did Rose Mary Woods say she made part of the buzz?"

"She didn't know the tape recorder was possessed. She

thought she had caused the buzz by putting her foot on the pedal. But the experts proved that you can't erase a tape on the Uher 5000 with your foot. It has to be done by hand. Who else but the devil would have this information?'' Dr. Damien said.

"What can be done now?" I asked.

"We have to get the devil out of the machine."

"You mean exorcise it?"

"Exactly. It's going to be a tough battle, but it has to be done."

"How do you exorcise the devil from a Uher 5000?"

"First, you heat up water in a caldron until it is boiling. Then you throw in white papers on ITT and the milk fund and stir. Add IRS tax returns and three strands of Howard Hughes' mustache. Throw in a dash of Magruder, a sprig of Stans and a cup of Colson.

"Keep the pot boiling and recite the following:

Haldeman, Erlichman, Mitchell and Dean
The tapes will show the Prez is clean.
If they don't, the story goes,
The hum was made by Rose Mary's toes.

"Then," said Dr. Damien, "take the Uher 5000 and throw it in the boiling water until the recording head melts."

"And that will exorcise the devil in the tape machine?"

"It should," Dr. Damien replied.

"What if we go to all this trouble and it turns out Satan was not involved and that somebody in the White House *had actually* erased the tapes?"

"Impossible," said Dr. Damien. "The devil would never stand for it."

WOULD YOU GO TO JAIL?

The Rose Mary Woods tape incident has raised a great moral issue in this country: How far should a secretary go to protect her boss?

I posed this question to my secretary, Ellie Cobey. "Ellie," I asked her, "would you lie for me to keep me out of jail?"

"I do it all the time," she replied.

"I don't mean *that* kind of lying," I said. "I mean if I committed a high crime or a misdemeanor."

"That's the only kind of lying I do for you," she said. "Like when you're taking a nap and I tell people you're in conference, or when you've taken some beautiful girl to lunch and I tell your wife that you're at the Watergate hearings. Or when someone calls and asks you to address a Lions Club and I tell them you're going to be in Tucson. I can't remember a time when I haven't lied for you."

"All secretaries do that," I said, "I mean *really* lie. Suppose I tape recorded a conversation I had with Frank Sinatra in which he told me his personal thoughts about Maxine Cheshire, and these tapes were subpoenaed. Would you erase those tapes for me?"

"You mean by pressing the play button and the record button at the same time?" she asked.

"If you couldn't erase it with your foot, yes."

"Wouldn't that produce a hum?" she wanted to know.

"Possibly," I said. "But we could explain away the hum by pointing out that you had your electric typewriter and a lamp on at the same time."

"It sounds rather farfetched to me," she said.

"That's not the point. The point is would you, as my personal secretary, be willing to get on a stand and swear under oath that to the best of your knowledge the erasure of that particular tape was an accident?"

"Are you asking if I'd commit perjury for you?"

"Well, if you want to be technical about it, yes."

"Couldn't I refuse to testify on the grounds that it would incriminate me?" she asked.

"You could," I said, "but that would not be showing much candor. I think because of my position it's important that all the truth come out. If you're going to take it upon yourself to erase tapes to protect me, I think you should be willing to pay the price for it."

"That wasn't the question," she protested.

"Ellie, even if you are my secretary, I can't condone a crime that you have committed."

"Are you trying to tell me that if I perjured myself to help you, you wouldn't protect me?" she said.

"Ellie, this is a land of laws, not of people. No matter what your motives were, the position of trust I hold would demand that I see that justice is done."

"Does that mean I would have to go to jail?"

"Ellie, jail isn't that bad. Some of our best people are going to jail for perjury."

She started to cry. "I don't know how I got into this."

"It's all right, Ellie," I said, trying to console her. "We all make mistakes. The important thing is to be big enough to admit them and take your punishment. I'll forget we had this conversation, unless of course I'm impeached."

A HUMDINGER EXPLANATION

It seems the mystery of the 18½-minute hum on one of the key Presidential tapes may never be resolved. Rose Mary Woods, President Nixon's lawyers and even Judge Sirica have no idea how it happened. Every possible theory has been advanced and rejected—except one.

The one explanation that no one has mentioned is that the President was humming by himself for the entire 18½ minutes.

I was put on to this theory by a former White House aide who says that one of President Nixon's biggest secrets is that he likes to hum when he's struggling with the major problems of the world.

"You mean the entire eighteen and a half minutes of hum on the tape could have been made by the President?" I asked.

"Easily. I've seen the President hum for hours at a time. It relaxes him and helps him tough it out. He hummed all during the Vietnam War, and I wouldn't be surprised if he's been humming ever since Watergate."

"But if the eighteen and a half minutes of humming was made by the President, why didn't he just say so and save us all from thinking the worst?"

"Because the President doesn't want anyone to know he hums. He'll do anything to keep people from finding out."

"But why?" I asked.

"He is afraid if the American people know he hums, they

may think he's not cool. He doesn't want to go down in history as the first American President who was known as a nervous hummer."

"There's nothing wrong with humming. Lots of people do it."

"Yes, but the President doesn't hum very well. If you listen to the disputed tape, you'll realize his voice is a terrible monotone. Can you imagine what the media would do to him if they discovered the eighteen-and-a-half-minute hum on the tape was actually made by the President of the United States?"

"Then you think Rose Mary Woods was aware that the hum she heard was made by her boss?"

"I'm certain of it. She's been trying to break him of the humming habit for twenty-five years."

"What about the President's lawyers? Did they know?"

"I'm not certain of that. The President only hums around people he really trusts. When he goes out boating with Bebe Reboze, he hums, and when he screens *Patton* with his family, he hums, and when he watches the Redskins, he hums."

"Wait a minute. On the tape there were two distinctive hums. One went for five minutes and was very loud, and the rest of the time the hum was much lower. How do you explain that?"

"The President was probably doing two different things. He may have hummed loudly when he was reading the Washington *Post,* and he could have hummed softly while he was working on his income taxes."

"Of course," I said, "that explains it. And to think Rose Mary Woods is taking the rap for the hum."

"That," said the White House aide, "is what secretaries are for."

FIRE IN THE WHITE HOUSE

The key word that keeps popping up in the transcripts of the Presidential tapes is "scenario." The President and his aides kept coming up with a scenario for every setback in the Watergate case.

The one scenario they never constructed, and the most vital one in my opinion, is what they should have done when Alexander Butterfield disclosed the President had taped everyone who came into the Oval Office. If I had been the President's trusted adviser, this is how I would have handled it. I'll be B and the President will be P.

B: Mr. President, Butterfield just blew the whistle on the tapes.

P: ("Oh fudge" deleted)

B: I think we'd better game plan this right away.

P: ("Gee willikers!" deleted) What do you suggest we do?

B: They're going to demand those tapes. You can bet your sweet (inaudible) on that. We have the following options: (A) We turn them over; (B) we refuse to turn them over; or (C) we have a fire in the White House basement.

P: Tell me about "C."

B: Yes, sir. It's late at night, and you're up in the bedroom, and Mrs. Nixon says she smells smoke. You tell her Kissinger is probably burning some old cables.

P: ("Golly gumdrops!" deleted) Suppose the butler comes in and says he smells smoke also?

B: You tell him to mind his own (expletive deleted) business and go back to bed.

P: Hmmmm. You know there are a ("heckuva" deleted) lot of tapes in the basement. What happens when the fire department is called? They could put out the fire right away and save the tapes.

B: You stonewall them in the Rose Garden and tell them how proud you are of the fire fighters of America and how much it means to you to have them come to the White House at that hour in the morning. We'll get Pat Buchanan to write up a little speech for you to deliver in which you point out the difference between fire departments of the United States and those in the enslaved countries of the world that you have been to.

P: What are the differences?

B: In America every local community can choose its own

fire-fighting equipment, and the government does not dictate what type of trucks they should order. If a community wants a hook and ladder, they can order a hook and ladder. If they decide they'd rather have a pumper, it's their option.

P: So while I'm reading the speech, the fire in the basement is going full blast?

B: Right. Now for safety, what we ought to do is have you present each fireman with a scroll expressing the gratitude of every man, woman and child in this nation for the wonderful work they are doing. You could personally sign each one in front of them. This should give us enough time to burn up every tape you ever made.

P: ("Yippee dee doo da!" deleted) I could go on television the next day and say how distraught I am that these tapes, which would have proved my innocence, once and for all, have gone up in smoke and have been lost to history. But I can promise to turn over all my notes of those conversations which will show I knew nothing about Watergate or the cover-up. Without the tapes we've got the darn Watergate committee by the ("cat's whiskers" deleted). Good work, Art. Oh, there is one more thing. How did the fire start in the first place?

B: John Dean was sneaking a smoke in the basement instead of doing what you asked him to do. And he threw his butt on the tapes.

P: (Laughter) I like it. Let's see how it plays in ("blinkety" deleted) Peoria.

HOW THEY DID IT

We know a lot about the Presidential transcripts now, but we still do not know much about how they were transcribed. A friend of mine who was at the White House told me the story involved with getting out the 1,308 pages and 200,000 words in time for the President's speech.

This, according to him, is what happened.

"We got the word that the President had decided to turn

over transcripts of the tapes to the House Judiciary Committee, and the call went out for thirty secretaries who could type and listen to tapes at the same time."

"Why didn't they ask Rose Mary Woods to transcribe them?" I asked.

"She's not very good at using a tape machine. And we didn't want to go through that whole dreary explanation again about why long portions of the tape were erased."

"Did you hurt her feelings when you told her she couldn't do it?"

"She was rather miffed at first, but to make it up to her, we let her type the speech the President gave on TV explaining why the transcripts would show he was innocent."

"So then what happened?"

"We set up a room in the bottom of the White House with tape machines, typewriters, coffee and Danish.

"We explained to the girls that they were part of history and what they typed could make or break the President of the United States."

"Wow, that must have really scared them," I said.

"We told them that they would be locked in for the weekend and work eight-hour shifts. We had set up cots in John Dean's old office where they could catch up on sleep when they weren't working."

"Dean would have liked that," I said.

"The first shift started typing at midnight on Friday. In the beginning the girls thought it would be a lark, but as they started listening to the tapes, some of them went white. One girl said to me, 'This must be the wrong tape. Someone's cursing on it.' I told her it was the right tape and that the voice they heard was the President cursing. She didn't believe me and thought I was joking, so I made a speech to all the girls.

"I told them they would hear a lot of foul language on the tapes, but these were really code words the President used for national security reasons. I instructed them to type in an 'expletive deleted' or an 'inaudible' when they heard a bad word. Otherwise, the Russians would be able to break our code."

"They accepted that?" I asked.

"They did at first, but pretty soon it started to get to them.

Several of them broke down and started to cry, so we had to send in new girls every half hour. The language was too much for them.

"One girl said, 'It isn't the expletives or the inaudibles that bother me. I've heard them before. But it's the unintelligibles that I just can't take.'

"By Saturday afternoon, the girls were refusing to type the transcripts and I was starting to worry. Then I got a brilliant idea if I must say so myself."

"What did you do?"

"I called up Billy Graham and asked him if he would come right over. He did, and I explained the problem to him. He understood it right away and said he would help."

"How?"

"He gave absolution to all the girls transcribing the tapes. He also told them, 'If God didn't want a President to curse, He would have never created Sony recording machines.'"

XII. WRITE YOUR OWN COLUMN

WHAT DID HENRY GIVE?

No one is quite certain what kind of deals Henry Kissinger made to get a settlement in the Middle East, but President Nixon probably is finding out.

I can imagine a scene at a great reception given by President Sadat of Egypt where leaders from all the Arab lands have gathered to meet the President of the United States. Henry is standing next to President Nixon in the receiving line and introducing the Arabs to the President.

"Mr. President," Henry says, "this is Sheikh Kaleli Abrim."

Sheikh Abrim shakes hands with Mr. Nixon. "My father sends his respects and asks me to thank you on behalf of our family for giving us the state of Rhode Island."

President Nixon appears startled and whispers to Henry, "Did we give Rhode Island to the Abrim family?"

Henry whispers back, "They wanted California, but I talked them into taking Rhode Island instead."

"What did we get in exchange?" the President asks.

"A steady, two-year supply of oil at fourteen dollars a barrel."

"Hmmm," the President says, "I guess nobody will mind losing Rhode Island."

The sheikh moves on, and Henry introduces the next Arab leader.

"This, Mr. President, is Hakim Assou, the Egyptian minister of public works."

Mr. Assou bows. "It is a great honor I finally meet the noble benefactor of Egypt."

"What did we give *them*?" the President whispers to Henry.

Henry replies, "The Ford Motor Company."

"In Egypt?" the President asks.

Henry blushes. "The Ford Motor Company in the United States. You see, in order to get a settlement in Syria we needed help from the Egyptians. The only way we could get help from them was to give them something in exchange. I thought the Ford Motor Company would be a nice *quid pro quo.*"

"Has anyone told Henry Ford?"

"Not yet. I didn't want it to leak to the press."

Mr. Assou moves on, and Henry introduces Fata Fatima, the leader of a splinter Maoist Palestinian guerrilla band.

Fatima refuses to shake hands with the President. He tells Henry, "I have been talking with my brothers, and we have decided you tricked us when you offered us three squadrons of Phantom jets. We will not go to Geneva unless we receive three nuclear submarines."

"What the devil?" the President says to Henry.

Henry whispers, "Don't pay any attention to him. He's all talk. They'll take the three squadrons of Phantom jets."

"Are you sure we want to give these people Phantom jets?"

"I had to give them *something,*" Henry says defensively.

The next Arab leader is Aleki Mossad, the Syrian minister of tourism.

"Oh, Great One," Mossad says, "you have saved the Syrian tourist industry."

The President looks questioningly at Henry.

Henry says, "I forgot to tell you last week. In order to get the Syrians off the Golan Heights I promised them Las Vegas. We have to sign the deed after lunch."

Before the President can meet the next Arab leader, President Sadat tells Mr. Nixon he has an urgent call from Golda Meir.

After five minutes a rather upset President returns to the receiving line. He whispers to Henry, "Did you give Israel the Standard Oil Company of New Jersey?"

"Come to think of it," Henry says, "I did. Originally they demanded Alaska, but I told them it was out of the question."

THE FRENCH DON'T UNDERSTAND

The good news from France is that the French no longer hate Americans. If anything, they are very sympathetic with President Nixon's plight and cannot understand what all the fuss in Washington is about.

My good friend François said to me, "*Alors, mon vieux,* what are you doing to your poor President?"

"Nothing really, François. It's just that he's in a slight jam and they're trying to find out whether they should impeach him or not."

"But what did he do?" François asked.

"It's hard to explain. You see there were some people working for his reelection who decided to find out what the other political party was doing by bugging its headquarters."

"*Mais oui,*" François said, "what is wrong with that?"

"It wasn't just a question of bugging the opposition's office. They also discovered that people working for the President had large amounts of cash which they were using to sabotage the President's opponents."

"*Naturellement.* What else would they do if they were trying to beat the other party?"

"You don't understand, François. What they were doing was illegal."

"I understand perfectly," François said rather irritably. "But what is wrong with doing something illegal to win an election?"

"Well, it wasn't just a question of the President's people doing something illegal. It turned out that when the people involved were arrested, an effort was made to cover up the crime so nobody would know anyone in the White House had anything to do with it."

"*Je comprends,* any politician in France would do the same thing," François said.

"The cover-up, as far as we know," I continued, "involved a former Attorney General the head of the FBI and several people very high in the administration. All sorts of evidence was destroyed, and some of the President's most trusted men perjured themselves before the Senate Watergate Committee and the grand jury."

"We read all this in the French newspapers. But you still haven't answered my question. What did they do wrong?"

"François, how can I make you understand? There was one political scandal after another. The Vice President of the United States was forced to resign for taking bribes. The White House kept an enemies list which they were going to use to get people who criticized the President. They also hired 'plumbers' to break into people's homes and offices. One thing led to another, and pretty soon there was some question of whether the President of the United States himself was involved."

"In France we would have been very disappointed if our President wasn't involved."

"Then there were other scandals. Mr. Nixon forgot to pay four hundred and sixty-five thousand dollars in income taxes."

"*Vive la Nixon,*" François said.

"Then it was discovered that the President had tape-recorded everyone who came into his office. Some of the tapes could prove whether he was involved in the cover-up of the other crimes. The House of Representatives and the special prosecutor asked to hear all the tapes, but Mr. Nixon gave them only a few which he claimed were sufficient to find out if he was guilty or not."

"Any Frenchman would do the same thing. You have told me nothing so far to explain why you keep picking on him."

"François, I didn't want to tell you this, but the tapes

revealed that the President of the United States puts catsup on his cottage cheese."

François' eyes bugged out. "*Alors*, why didn't you say that before? Now I understand why you want to impeach him."

THE CONVERSION OF COLSON

When Charles Colson got religion, the first person he wanted to break the news to was his grandmother—the very same grandmother he had vowed to run over in 1972 to get Richard Nixon reelected President.

He knocked on the door and cried, "Granny, it's me, Charles."

"You go away, Charley," his grandmother said, "and take your car with you."

"Granny, you don't understand. I'm not here to run over you. I've got religion now. I've come to pray with you."

Colson's grandmother opened the door a couple inches. "You're joshing me, Charley boy."

"It's true, Granny, I'm no longer the mean, dirty, rotten, unscrupulous trickster you used to bounce on your knee. I've been reborn, Granny."

She hesitated. "How do I know this ain't one of your tricks to get me out in the street so you can go vroom, vrooooomm with your motor again?"

"I have Senator Harold Hughes with me. He'll tell you I mean it."

"That's right, Granny," Senator Hughes said. "Charley has made his peace, and he's asking everyone to forgive him his sins."

"I ain't so sure I'm ready to forgive him. You know I was flat on my back for six months after the 1972 election."

"Granny, please let me in. I want to show you I'm a new man."

"All right," Colson's grandmother said, "but leave your car keys out on the stoop."

Colson came into the house with Senator Hughes.

"Shall we kneel together?" Colson asked.

"Not me," his grandmother replied. "I haven't been able to kneel since you screamed at me, 'Four more years!' and then put your Oldsmobile into drive."

"That's all in the past, Granny. As a matter of fact I've pleaded guilty and I'm going to be a witness against Nixon."

"Don't blame you for that. I read the transcripts, and it turns out the President didn't think too much of you. He called you a name-dropper and used to laugh at you with Dean, Ehrlichman and Haldeman. My, Charley, I never thought anyone would play you for a sucker the way Nixon did."

"I have to forgive him, too, Granny. Since my conversion I can feel no animosity toward anyone, not even the President of the United States."

"By gum, Charley, you really may be a changed man. It's hard for me to believe, of course, after what I've been through."

"I want to make it up to you, Granny. I want to cleanse my soul. The devil was in me in 1972. You understand that, don't you?"

"I understand it, because you're my grandson. But what about all the other people you played dirty tricks on? What about the political ads and the forged telegrams and the enemies list?"

"I'm going to become a government witness, Granny, and make amends. I'm going to tell the truth, the whole truth and nothing but the truth."

"So help you God," Senator Hughes added.

"Anybody want any cider?" Colson's grandmother asked.

"No, we've got to be going. We have miles to go before we sleep. All I want to know, Granny, is, do you forgive me?"

"All right, Charley, I forgive you. But no more getting involved in Presidential campaigns, you hear?"

Colson smiled for the first time. "Cross my heart and hope to die."

IMPEACHING CONGRESS

"Congressman Cheesedip, how do you feel about the Watergate affair?"

"I am shocked, appalled and horrified that such a thing could happen in this great land of ours."

"What is Congress doing to prevent future Watergates from taking place?"

"We are studying the matter very closely."

"Do you believe there is any possibility that the House will pass serious election-reform legislation this year?"

"I didn't understand the question."

"Congressman Cheesedip, what I meant was that although most members of the House are very critical of every aspect of Watergate, they seem to be dragging their feet when it comes to making the elections in this country less corrupt."

"I will not accept that. We have been thinking about election reform for some time now. We have been talking about it for more than a year. How can you say we're dragging our feet?"

"Mainly because you haven't done anything."

"Well, I would like to say this. Reforming election campaigns is a very serious matter. We have to look at it from all sides. It's true that there have been abuses, particularly in the area of financing political candidates, and we're very concerned about this. At the same time it would be a mistake if we abolished these abuses and made it more difficult for men of high principle to run."

"Then, Congressman Cheesedip, could I say that you are against election reforms this year?"

"I am not against election reforms. I take the position—and I have said this publicly many times—that we must have reforms in our political process. But I believe it would be a very dangerous thing to pass any laws that would make it more difficult for well-meaning people to contribute to a political campaign. Their voices should be heard, and if they want to do it by financing a particular candidate then I say God bless them. That's the American way of doing things."

"But isn't that the very thing that got the Committee for the Re-Election of the President in all its trouble?"

"I don't think we should be tarred by what the Committee for the Re-Election of the President did. I am proud to say that although I have received contributions from the milk producers, the oil companies and the construction industries, I have never permitted this to interfere in how I would vote on any particular bill. Every Congressman on this Hill feels the same way. If we didn't, we would of course ask for stronger election laws."

"Aren't you afraid, Congressman Cheesedip, that if you don't pass some reform legislation you will be impeached?"

"What are you talking about?"

"The Constitution provides that every two years the American people can impeach a Congressman by voting him out of office."

"That's outrageous. You have to prove he's guilty of a high crime or a misdemeanor."

"No you don't. All you have to prove is that the Congressman did nothing about corruption in government. Any voter will tell you that's an impeachable offense."

"Hmmrummf, I thought you wanted to talk to me about Watergate."

A GREAT YEAR FOR W.I.

Watergate Industries held its annual stockholders meeting at the federal courthouse in Washington last week, and Sherlock Springbinder, the chairman of the board, reported a windfall profit of $2 billion. Watergate Industries is a conglomerate that deals in all aspects of the Watergate affair from providing legal talent to selling memoirs of Watergate personalities.

Mr. Springbinder told the happy stockholders, "The way things are going, Watergate should be one of the best growth stocks of 1974. The legal profession alone has earned thirty million dollars and very few of the trials have begun. By the time all the indictments are handed down we expect to have thirty thousand lawyers working full time on motions. After the trials we will have another five thousand producing appeals. Estimated net income from this division should bring in a hundred million dollars."

There was a great deal of applause.

"Our book division is also showing a great profit. We estimate that everyone involved in Watergate from John Dean to the mail room boy at the Committee for the Re-Election of the President will have a nonfiction or fiction book out by next Christmas. If you include newspapermen, defendants, prosecutors, former White House personnel, former Attorneys General, milk producers, ex-CIA men, secretaries and grand jury foremen, we believe there will be six hundred and seventy thousand different books published this year, and the advances alone will come to twenty million dollars. If President Nixon decides to write his book of what really happened, I could see another ten million dollars in added revenue."

There was more applause.

"The movie rights for Watergate are going very briskly. Robert Redford is working on *All the President's Men*, and several other movie producers are readying projects, including *Gidget Goes to the Watergate, Last Tango at the White House, The Tapes of Wrath, Lassie at the Supreme Court, The Life of Bebe Rebozo* and *Confessions of a Jesuit Priest*.

"Watergate Industries has bought four movie studios, and we now have a record division where we intend to produce the hit expletives from the transcripts."

Springbinder continued: "We also plan to go into TV in a big way if the impeachment trial takes place. We will produce *Monday Night at the Senate* with Howard Cosell and Frank Gifford, *To Tell the Truth* with Richard Nixon, *I've Got a Secret* starring Gordon Liddy and the *Six Million Dollar Man* with Maurice Stans.

"Watergate Industries is happy to announce it is going into the employment agency business, since it is estimated that there will be three hundred forty-five thousand eight hundred and ninety White House aides looking for jobs in the next twelve months.

"Our Congressional subpoena printing plant is now working twenty-four hours a day, and we just received a multimillion-dollar contract from the House Judiciary Committee which should keep us busy for two more years."

Springbinder got a standing ovation.

"Are there any questions?" he asked.

"Why aren't there more women involved with Watergate?" a militant stockholder shouted from the floor.

Springbinder answered nervously, "It's true that Watergate

was strictly a white male affair, with very few exceptions. We tried to find women who could become involved, but there just weren't any who were qualified. Women don't seem to be physiologically or mentally able to cope with all it takes to be part of a Watergate scandal.''

WRITE YOUR OWN COLUMN

The mailman keeps coming in every day delivering letters which indicate the country is polarizing on the impeachment issue. The Nixon supporters blame the whole thing on the press. The Nixon detractors say the press hasn't been tough enough. What to do?

As someone who is always trying to please everyone, I believe I have a solution. I got it from the "inaudibles" on the Presidential tapes. This column is the first one printed in a newspaper which will take care of both the pro-Nixon and anti-Nixon forces. You fill in the blanks any way you want to, which should satisfy everyone's desire for fairness.

Richard M. Nixon is probably the greatest _____ in American history. He began his political life as a _____. When he was Senator, Dwight Eisenhower chose him to be his Vice President. After working with Mr. Nixon for several years, Eisenhower thought he was _____.

Mr. Nixon ran for governor of California in 1962. When he was defeated, he vowed he would _____. In 1968 he ran for President of the United States on the Republican ticket. At that time he promised the American people to _____ and _____ and _____. After being elected President, he was able to _____ and _____ and _____.

In 1972 President Nixon decided to run again. To assure his reelection he told his staff to _____. The staff, determined to show their loyalty to the President, took off after the Democratic hopefuls by _____. They went so far as to _____.

Mr. Nixon was _____ of what they were doing.

The organization set up to make sure Mr. Nixon would win

was the Committee for the Re-Election of the President. It raised $_____ million. Some of this money was given by _____, some of it came from _____, and a lot of it was raised in cash by _____.

At this point in time, five men were arrested breaking into Democratic headquarters at the Watergate. When President Nixon heard about it on _____, he was _____.

The Watergate break-in led to a series of investigations by the FBI, the Senate and a federal grand jury. When the results of these investigations were brought to the President's attention, he immediately _____. Then he _____ with members of his staff.

Conflicting testimony by members of the White House staff led eventually to an impeachment inquiry by the House. The key evidence, as it turned out, did not come from John Dean, who is a _____, but from tapes of conversations between the President and his staff. The President said these tapes were _____, but the special prosecutor and the House Judiciary Committee said they were _____.

Under great pressure, the White House finally released transcripts of the tapes which showed the President to be _____ in the Watergate affair. They also indicated that President Nixon was a man of _____ character.

The President's lawyers announced that they would not provide any further evidence for the impeachment proceedings. This has led some people to think the President is _____ and other people to think he is _____.

There is no doubt in anybody's mind that the President will be found _____ of the charges made against him.

In any case we can expect the _____ media to _____ President Nixon until the issue is resolved.

Now if this column doesn't satisfy *everyone,* then I'm going to Paris.

XIII. EPILOGUE

A VISIT WITH CHECKERS

When President Nixon dropped his latest bombshell on the American people, I was so shaken up I didn't know what to do. So I went to the graveside of Checkers, the Nixons' cocker spaniel, and sat on the stone.

"Well, Checkers," I said, "your master has had it. He's either got to resign or they're going to kick him out of office. You saved him once, but you can't save him this time. . . . I know what you're saying, 'How could it happen? How could a man who had the whole world in his hands blow it the way he did?' I can't answer that.

"He did some great things, Checkers, even his worst enemies acknowledge that. He brought about a new relationship with China, and some sort of detente with Russia, and the whole world picture changed for the better under him.

"But at the same time he tore the fabric of his own country to shreds. First his people tried to steal an election, an election he was certain of winning without one bit of skulduggery. Then he tried to cover up the crimes of the people who worked for him—cheap, crummy crimes that a fifth rate politician would consider beneath him.

"Why, Checkers, why?

"That's the question we'll be asking for years to come. Why would a man with the power and the glory of the Presidency become involved with dirty tricks, housebreaking, obstruction of justice, and perjury? I'm not making this up, Checkers. It's all in the tapes. . . . Oh, you don't know about the tapes? Well, you see, soon after your master took over the Presidency he decided to record the conversations of everyone he came in contact with—without their knowledge, except for H. R. Haldeman. You don't know Haldeman? He was Mr. Nixon's closest aide—he ran the White House with John Ehrlichman—they've both been indicted for the same crimes that finally caught up with your master.

"Anyway, the tapes were the only evidence that could convict Mr. Nixon, and he turned some over to the justice people, and he was ordered to turn over other tapes by the courts. I know what you're going to ask, 'Why didn't he burn the tapes?' Nobody knows the answer to that question, Checkers. Either he was stupid or he was so contemptuous of the laws of this country he didn't believe anyone would ever get to hear them. Once he was ordered to turn over the tapes that implicated him, his goose was cooked.

"But do you want to know the worst thing your master did? He lied to the American people. He lied to his friends, his lawyers, his own party, and everyone who believed in him.

"Why, Checkers, why? You knew him better than we did. Why would a man think the American people would keep him in office after he deceived them time and time again?

"Was it scorn for us that made him do it? Was it some insecurity in his character that kept him from playing by the rules? Or was it simply a case of a man who was a born loser even when he became President of the United States?

"Well, I've got to be going now. The country will survive, Checkers. We're much better than your master thinks we are. And we do have some consolation. If things hadn't worked out the way they did, Agnew might have become President and then we would have had to impeach him."